My Journey Into Native America

Behind the dreamcatchers

By

Dave Jones

Best Wishes

Dave Jones

Contact the writer at:

books.davejones@gmail.com

INTRODUCTION

I've had an interest in all things Native American for a number of years. I wouldn't go as far as to say an obsession, more a curiosity. As an Englishman viewing this subject, I do so from a distance. All I knew prior to my visits was what was fed to me, mostly by White America.

I decided to dig a little deeper. I wanted to see things from the side of the Indians. So that's exactly what I did.

My story is in two parts, in part 1 my wife and I take a road trip travelling around the mid-west, taking in places of significance. Done mostly with the assistance of our Native American guides, we build a foundation of knowledge that was previously limited to say the least.

Part 2, I return alone to spend time with one of our original guides, somebody that I became good friends with. Reuben FastHorse introduces me to modern day life for the indigenous people of America. I get to meet his friends and family along with people and places of importance within the community. My eyes have been opened.

Through reading my story, you will learn what I have learnt. Through the pages of this book, I will share with you my experiences and hopefully you will understand what drove me to write this in the first place.

I hope you enjoy.

PART ONE

CHAPTER ONE

CHRISTOPHER COLUMBUS DAY

TODAY is Monday the 12th October 2015, Christopher Columbus Day. When I awoke this morning, I was not aware that such a holiday existed. As it has no significance to my everyday life back in the U.K, there is no reason why I would be. This year however, it is different, very different.

I am stood at the foot of the mass grave of American Indians at the site of the Wounded Knee massacre on the Pine Ridge Reservation in South Dakota. The sun is shining and although warm, there is a strong breeze that carries a cool air. I stand beside my wife and our Lakota guide (now friend) Reuben FastHorse. There is silence as we look at the grave along with the other headstones that surround it. We look out at the open fields around us, each long blade of the yellowy green grass dances and sways in the wind. This seemingly unspoilt land, that in my eyes is tinged with red, the red from the blood of those innocent people that were put to their death at the hands of the white man. Some being left lying in the snow for as long as four days until being gathered up and put into the pit that we are now standing just a couple of feet away from.

A young Lakota boy rides up on his bicycle, he is maybe 9 or 10 years old. He says "hello" and we return his greeting. Reuben asks him if there is no school today and the boy reminds us that it is a holiday and the schools are closed. He offers to sell us some strips of material that hang from his handlebars, we decline. Around the grave there are prayer ties and other offerings that visitors have left, I realise later that this is what the boy was selling. A few moments pass before his friend arrives and they leave together.

Later in the day I think about the boy and I wish now that I had spent more time speaking to him. I wonder how he sees his future, what he wants to be when he grows up? If I had bought the prayer ties from him, what would he have spent the money on? Would he have spent it on himself, maybe buying candy or would he have given it to his mother in-order to help feed the family? Perhaps his mother sent him. I guess I will never know.

When Christopher Columbus first set foot on American soil on the 12th October 1492, nobody could have envisioned what lay ahead. Yet with some strange irony, I stand here at the site of the Wounded Knee massacre on the day the rest of America celebrates his arrival on these shores with an extra day off of work. I doubt that the people of Pine Ridge share their joy.

Prior to the arrival of Columbus, many tribes knew of America as Turtle Island. Some, although not many, may still refer to it as such. Also, there are a few that still have issues with the terminology 'Indians' and 'Native Americans', for as they see it, their ancestors existed long before any such concept. To these people, the preferred name is First Nation or Indigenous People. However, as this is a small minority, and the people that I have been most involved with are comfortable with these words, as much as I hope I do not cause offence, I shall be using them throughout my story. I'll also be using the words 'whites' and 'white man'.

So, where did the name 'Indians' come from in the first place? The term 'Indians' came about because Columbus actually thought he had arrived in India, however, he was clearly a long way off with his calculations. The people of America claim that Columbus discovered this great land, the Native Americans like to spin that on its head, believing that they, actually-discovered Christopher Columbus.

The events at Wounded Knee on the 29th December 1890 hold their place in the history books as one of the worst atrocities inflicted upon the Indians, although there were many. The American Government were becoming restless with the ongoing Ghost Dance that the people were partaking in, mistaking it for a war dance. The Indians believed that their spiritual ceremony would relieve them of the whites, that the settlers would vanish, and their hunting grounds would return to how they once were. A scuffle broke out when a soldier attempted to take a Lakota man's rifle. During the altercation, a single shot rang out. Immediately on hearing this the seventh cavalry opened fire on the Indians, very few were spared. Some 250-300 men, women and children were massacred. Today we hold a respectful silence in a peaceful, tranquil setting. The sounds and sights of that day, a complete contrast to this. With children's blood on the clothes of their desperate, screaming mothers, people gripped with fear try to run, to find some sort of an escape route. There isn't one. The fate of these people had been determined. Not by a court of law but by the men representing the United States Government stood, in military uniforms, before them.

It goes without saying that visiting such a place is a moving experience. It stirs me emotionally to the point where I do not just think of the injustice, I feel it. The spirits of these victims find their way into my soul and although on the outside I remain composed, inside, my heart is crying. How could something so wrong be allowed to happen?

With the wind that blows around us come the images that pass through my mind. The horrific sights that would have been witnessed. The heartbreak of seeing your loved ones fall knowing that you were soon to follow. As the breeze dies down, the images fade and I switch back to the here and now. At this moment, it would be good to be able to grab on to a positive. To think that life has improved for the Lakota people in the time that has passed. Lessons must have been learned, right? Things must be so much better now, musn't they? The saddest thing of all was the drive we took through Pine Ridge to get here. Some 125 years on from this fatal day, the torture of the Native Americans continues. Maybe not with bullets and guns but through poor living conditions and poverty.

CHAPTER TWO

PINE RIDGE

Originally, visiting Pine Ridge was not on our agenda, it was added last minute. I'm glad that it was as I wanted to see all things, good and bad. I wanted to take away as much as I could from this trip. So, what have I taken away from my time on Pine Ridge? Among other things, a hunger to find out more.

As an outsider looking in, I have always been of the belief that the worst areas affected by poverty in America are inner city ghettos with high afro-carribean and Mexican populations. Indian reservations had previously not even entered my thoughts. To find out that these are in-fact the poorest places does not shock me as a statistic, yet the idea that it's so little known is astounding.

We are influenced by what we see on our television/movie screens and by the media in general, almost to the point of brainwashing. Modern day life on a reservation is not something that you would see in any regularity, anywhere. Why is this? Sadly, I do not have a definitive answer, although I do have my suspicions.

America, in my opinion, has a guilt complex regarding the Indians. When we feel guilty we tend to do one of two things, we either do everything we can to try to right our wrongs or we do nothing. We pretend that the problem does not exist. If we do not look at it, then it's

9

not there. Up until now, with devastating effects, America has opted for the latter. If they don't want to look at it, they certainly do not want the rest of the world looking at it. After all, America is the land of opportunity, right? From what I have seen, the American Dream for the Indians is nothing short of a nightmare.

For me, however, the secret is now out. I know that Pine Ridge is consistently either bottom or second from bottom on the poverty list. I know that the reservations are the toughest places to survive in America. I know this not because I have read it in a newspaper but because I have seen it with my own eyes.

I was told before we entered Pine Ridge that all is not good there. I was thankful of the warning. When you dig a little deeper you can find out all-of the statistics. You can see that Pine Ridge has the highest unemployment, lowest income, highest suicide rate, high-levels of alcoholism (even with the reservation being 'dry') and drug abuse. The average life expectancy for men is just 47. As I write this, I am 46 years old, one year away from being the average age to die, a horrifying thought.

The alcohol and drug abuse are serious issues when we look at the average life expectancy, so if Pine Ridge is dry (no alcohol) how can there be a problem? Clearly, it's very difficult to police. Where there's a will there's a way and if people are determined enough to do something, they will do it. The fact that just outside of the reservation, approximately two miles into Nebraska, there's a place called White Clay that consists of four liquor stores and not much else, doesn't help. White Clay has a population of just 14 people, yet these stores sell over 12000 cans of beer per day between them. (figures from 2009)

As we drive through White Clay we see plenty of desperate people. Some sat by the roadside in small groups, others roaming aimlessly. The reality is, they could do with a good meal rather than another drink, they look malnourished, hair unkempt with scruffy, dirty clothes. Before the arrival of Europeans, the Natives had no knowledge of alcohol. It was introduced to them by us. It is not something that they have taken to well and has become a problem of epidemic proportions. For the people that we see in White Clay, alcohol and drug addiction has them gripped. Sadly, their only objective in life is to seek their next drink or fix. If a car pulls up they approach it to ask for money. We do not stop.

A lot of the Indians would like to see White Clay closed-down. There is a belief among many that if the alcohol ban were to be lifted on the reservation, at least they would be in control of their own problem. The money from the selling of alcohol would be made by the Indians and could be used to set up rehabilitation centres, as opposed to the shop owners of White Clay getting rich off-of the back of troubled souls.

To visit Pine Ridge and White Clay is a depressing experience. To live there must be extremely so. Looking around you, in its current state, you cannot see where the inspiration for change can come from. Opportunities appear to be few and far between and you can understand why some choose to move to cities to become 'Urban Indians' in-order to make a better life for themselves. Although this appears to cause a little friction too. Wouldn't it be great if there were no need for people to move away to fulfil their ambitions, if they could achieve all they wanted on Pine Ridge?

Based on the lifestyle that I'm used to, I find one of the most distressing elements is the lack of things to do socially. There's a casino for adults and I've recently discovered that Levis have built a skate park for the youngsters. With the ban on alcohol, obviously there are no bars but how about a cinema, a decent leisure/sports centre, a bowling alley, an ice rink, a music venue etc, places where people can go with their friends? Whether these things would be desirable to the locals, I don't know. They may have other things on their wish list. What I do believe however, is that idle minds can lead to drink and drugs. The type of activities is not so important, in my opinion, to have some form of enjoyment and escapism away from alcohol is. These things would also create more jobs and bring more revenue to the area as well as give an improved social life to the residents.

A big problem for anyone looking to start a business on Pine Ridge is the lack of funds. Banks tend not to lend to people on the reservations as they see it as high-risk. This creates a bit of a catch 22 situation.

I have heard the words 'third world' and Pine Ridge mentioned in the same sentence many times. I am fortunate enough to have visited India (a country that automatically springs to mind when we think of third world) on numerous occasions throughout my life and although I can see why the comparisons are made, for me there is one fundamental difference. In India, wherever you travel you will see poverty on a large scale. People working hard to make enough for their next meal.

11

However, even with this, there is a strong heartbeat, a real busyness about the place. Although I believe that there is still a heartbeat within Pine Ridge, it's been suppressed for so long and is in definite need of change. How that comes and in which form is for the locals to decide. This should be debated with them to seek that brighter future.

CHAPTER THREE

WELCOME

When I set off on my journey there was no real purpose, it was based on curiosity and fascination. I never planned to write this book. I never even viewed it a journey as such. I knew that I was going on a tour, that was planned. The journey, however, was unexpected. I never thought for one moment that I would become so involved. As the title of the book suggests, I invite you to come along and experience the things that I've seen, to view it through my eyes.

As a personal trainer in my mid-forties from Southampton England (originally London), I guess that I'm an unlikely source of information on a subject that's set thousands of miles away. Sometimes in life, messages and messengers come in different guises.

Through writing this, I'm finding out new things on a daily-basis. Through each chapter, the aim is that you will do the same.

Taking a tour of all things Native American is far more than just a physical journey. With our own personal Indian guides taking us to many places of historical, spiritual and cultural interest, my wife Nickey and I couldn't have had a better experience.

By the end of our trip I was already thinking that, I now have all of this information inside me, all of these experiences to call on, all of these emotions stirring, what am I going to do with it? To get home and just put them to the back of my mind seemed wrong. I cannot un-see what I have seen. A month after returning home, these thoughts never faded. I wondered if there was anything that I could do to make a difference, even in the smallest of ways. That is when I began to write. On top of raising awareness of this subject, I'm also giving any profits made from sales of this book to Native American charities.

I found that I became consumed by this subject very quickly. It gripped me from day one of the trip, however, as you have now read the opening chapters, it's no longer just my journey, it's *our* journey, welcome aboard.

We arrive at Denver airport just as the sun is setting on a Thursday evening early October 2015. As soon as we disembark the plane, we feel as though we are entering Indian country. As anybody that has flown into Denver will know, as you walk from the aeroplane to baggage reclaim, Native American music plays softly through speakers and life size photographs of Native Americans line the walls. With most of the people surrounding us looking as though they are on business trips, wearing suits, laptops hanging on their shoulders, or children with their parents seemingly on family holidays, I doubt that anybody else arriving at the same time are here for the same reason as us. This gives the Native American flavour of the airport a personal feel, as though we have been treated to our own little welcoming ceremony.

We go through the usual security checks, get on a coach that takes us to our vehicle collection, pick up our car and head to our first hotel. After the long flight, it's nice to get to our beds. A good night sleep is needed as I know that the following morning I have my first of many long drives ahead.

CHAPTER FOUR

THE ROAD TO FORT LARAMIE

Over the course of our tour we drive more than 3000 miles. In the UK, any drive of significant distance may have you reaching for the Valium. Not here however. Once out of Denver, my time behind the wheel is stress free. Mile upon mile of open road in beautiful surroundings with just the occasional car or lorry for company. Colorado, Wyoming, South Dakota, Montana and very briefly Nebraska all to be ticked off of our list of States visited.

Our first full day has us heading to Fort Laramie, the first fort to be built along the Oregon Trail, originally put there by the fur traders. Over time it became more of a military base and was the place where the 1851 and 1868 treaties were signed.

So, this is it, Nickey, myself, a suitcase and the much-needed satnav all packed into a Ford Escape ready to hit the road. With our destination some five and a half hours away, we buckle up and set off.

The further we get from Denver, the more rural our surroundings become. Buildings by the roadside are being replaced by open fields, with just the odd house set back from the road with a mail box at the end of a long driveway, which more resembles a country lane than the entrance to a residential property.

City life quickly fades into a tiny dot in my rear-view mirror.

A couple of hours into our drive we pull over onto the grass verge to stretch our legs. In front of us, just the open road and fields, behind us, exactly the same. This is the first time in my life that I have experienced a complete, total silence out in the open. There's no sound at all. No cars nor lorries as far as our eyes can see. There are no people. It seems as though mother nature has taken the day off too as there's not even the sound of wind blowing or singing from the birds. It feels like we are the only ones on the planet. Almost post-apocalyptic. We could not be further from our everyday life back in England, and we love it.

Following our brief pit stop, we climb back into the car and continue on with the journey. It's getting close to lunchtime and the consideration of stopping for a bite to eat is soon to be at the forefront of our minds, the question is, where? "The next place we see, we stop," is the agreement. So, on we drive for what must be close to 100km (60ish miles) before eventually coming across a roadside diner/grill with the name 'Emporium' written on the front. Not quite an oasis in the desert but in comparison to the city life that we are use to, it certainly feels that way.

Emporium is a log cabin with a neon Budweiser sign lit up in the door window, just like in the movies. It's everything that we had hoped to see as part of our road trip.

We are, however, a little unsure of what to expect, as these places in the movies can throw up some odd characters. Who knows what or whom could be lurking behind the door? We are hungry and have no idea when the next place to eat will appear, so it's a chance we will have to take. We drive into the carpark somewhat apprehensively before going on in. As we enter we are greeted by the owners. I am relieved that they are nice, friendly people. I would guess they are in their early sixties and tell us that they moved here from Arizona a year before to run the diner. They seem as pleased to see us as we are to see them and genuinely interested in our trip. They tell us of other Brits that have used their facility, mostly bikers that have visited the Sturgis bike show that is held close by. They are allowed to ride this stretch of road with no crash helmets, so it has become popular for that reason.

The décor inside matches the wooden exterior, with sports and hunting memorabilia hanging from the walls. We love the place and the warm welcome that we receive makes us feel at home, instantly dismissing the concerns we had prior to entering. With so many positives it is essential that the food doesn't let them down. It certainly does not. The flame grilled cheeseburger is the best that I've ever eaten. We contemplate having the home-made apple pie for dessert but are both full so give it a miss. I'm sure it would have been lovely.

As we leave, the owners ask if we would mind writing a comment on the lean-to that is placed on the outside of the diner, along with other such messages from previous visitors. We are more than happy to oblige, so I take the pen and make a comment regarding the quality of the cheeseburger (it really was that good) along with our names and place of origin.

It seems fitting that our own little mark remains at a place that will always hold a soft spot in our memories.

With full stomachs, we continue-on to Fort Laramie.

Pulling into the carpark at the fort, we can see that there are only one or two other vehicles here, so clearly not many visitors today. As we climb out of the car, the silence hits us once more. This time it has an eerie feel, the type you only get in places of historic significance, as if figures from past generations are watching your every move. A creation of our imaginations maybe, yet something we both experience.

We approach the fort from the side and initially it looks like a few random buildings dotted here and there, some intact, some in ruins. The closer we get, the clearer the layout becomes. With the parade ground in the centre, the buildings are placed around the edge in a rectangular shape. Barracks, prison cells, kitchens and officer's residence all line the perimeter of the fort. We take a walk around and read the interesting information written on boards next to each building. This is all as you would expect it to be. The same format that you would see in most museums.

So why is Fort Laramie so important in our journey? Why is it important for us to visit? The simple answer is the treaties. These play such a big-role in the history of the Indians. The treaties have become famous, not for the reason they were put into place but for the fact that they have all been broken! All-of the promises made were worthless.

The treaty of 1851 was set between the U.S Government and representatives from Cheyenne, Crow, Sioux (Lakota), Arapaho, Mandan, Hidatsa, Assiniboine, Arikara tribes and was signed by all parties at the fort on the 17th September. It was agreed that the Government would pay a sum of $50,000 a year for fifty years, in return for the Indians allowing safe passage along the Oregon Trail for the people moving across country in search of their fortunes, more specifically, gold. Roads were to be built to make the travellers journey smoother. A Reservation was marked out for the Indians and no settlers nor travellers were allowed onto this land. As more gold was discovered in the west, the traffic increased and the less the conditions of the treaty were respected. With more and more regularity Indian lands were being encroached upon. The Government did nothing to prevent this happening, on top of that, the agreed compensation payments were not forth coming.

There you have it, a treaty, supposedly a legally binding contract, with nobody to ensure that it's upheld. This makes the agreement only of any value if the parties involved are honourable. One side clearly was not.

Having been deceived in 1851, when it came around to 1868 and yet another treaty, there was obviously far more scepticism on the part of the Indians.

So, on to the 1868 treaty; the Lakota tribe has seven bands, the Sicangu (Brule), Hunkpapa, Oglala, Mniconjou, Sihasapa, Itazipcho and Oohenunpa.

The Sicangu, Oglala, Mniconjou along with the Yanktonai Dakota and Arapaho signed this treaty. It was not signed by all-of the tribes because, quite simply, not all were in agreement. Many did not trust the white man.

Under Indian culture, no one man speaks for everyone. Each tribe has their own chiefs which speak for that group, however, the Government saw them all the same and a signature from one leader or chief was seen as an agreement by all.

The 1868 treaty saw the Indians handed ownership of the Black Hills (known to the Lakota people as Paha Sapa) along with hunting rights in South Dakota, Wyoming and Montana. No whites were to be allowed on the Powder River Country, the area between the Big Horn mountains and the Black Hills. The treaty also included financial incentives to encourage the Indians into farming and an English education system set up at missionary buildings, clearly put into place to convert the Indians to the European way of life. Once again, the promise of money for the land on which the Government wished to build roads and railroads was agreed.

If I were an Indian back then, looking at the contents of the treaty without the luxury of hindsight, I would probably have thought it looked pretty good. I may have objected to the enforcement of another culture onto my people but overall it looks reasonable. They get the sacred Black Hills, plenty of hunting ground and some money for the land that they were giving up. Considering the fact that some compromise was always going to be needed, the settlers were not going to just leave, I can understand why this would be signed.

On the flip side, it's just as easy to see why others were not convinced. Past experiences told them that the Government could not be trusted. Sadly, once again this proved to be the case. The reason...'There's gold in them thar hills'.

Gold discovered in the Black Hills led to a whole load of trouble over the coming years.

CHAPTER FIVE

SOUTH DAKOTA

After spending the night in Torrington, a small industrial town close to Fort Laramie, we rise early, shower, have breakfast and are on the road just as the sun is coming up. A beautiful red sky is our backdrop as we load the car ready to move on. Our journey today will be a leisurely one as we are not scheduled to do anything until the evening when we will be attending the Rapid City PowWow which is held annually. We are thrilled that it coincides with our visit and do not pass up the opportunity to go along and experience this gathering of Native Americans from around this area. We are looking forward to watching as they dance in full regalia and to hear the drums along with the singing of traditional songs.

We head out of Wyoming and into South Dakota and the Black Hills. It does not take long to fall in love with this state. It has so much natural beauty. Evergreen pine trees surround us as the road cuts like an incision through this national forest. Photographs taken from the Space Shuttle show that the Black Hills resemble the shape of a human heart. Some say, the heart of all of Mother Earth.

Amongst the beauty sits Mount Rushmore. Before leaving England, I had a battle with myself as to whether or not we should visit this famous landmark. To see the four ex-president's heads in the rock face. I've seen pictures of this many times and it's as much a symbol of America as the Statue of Liberty. Nickey is happy to go along with whatever I decide as she has a more 'along for the ride' attitude than one of being a major contributor to the planning of the trip. After much deliberation I decided that we would go there, for two reasons. Firstly, because we are so close so may as well take a look (this seems to be the view of many we speak to later). Secondly, so that I can bring to the attention of others, originally my family and friends, now to everybody reading this, that actually the whole thing is in pretty bad taste. This never crossed my mind until I started looking into our trip. Yes, as a spectacle it is quite impressive, yet, does it really belong here? The Black Hills are very important to the Indian people. After initially being given them as part of the 1868 treaty, once gold had been discovered, they were taken from them. To place this monument in a rock face right in the heart of their sacred land, of presidents that contributed to the breaking of treaties, is a real slap in the face for the people. At best, a severe lack of consideration for the feelings of the Indians. At worst, a deliberate humiliation of a past enemy.

I watch the other visitors basking in the glory of this part of American history. I don't believe that there is an intentional disregard of the Native Americans by these sight seers but, by all accounts, American schools tend to have a slanted view on this nation's history. Perhaps their reactions are only to be expected in relation to what they have been taught. Our time here is minimal.

From here we make our way to Rapid City, the second largest city after Sioux Falls in South Dakota. We arrive at the Country Inn Hotel at lunchtime, too early to check in as the room is still being cleaned from previous guests (we are not supposed to check in until 3pm). With the Powwow taking place in the city this weekend the staff are extremely busy yet work hard to get us into our room early all the same. In the mean-time we head next door to TGI Fridays to have some lunch and kill an hour.

As we make our way over, we can see a male of Latin American appearance in his mid-twenties. He's a very smart looking guy. Not a hair out of place, nice shirt, black jeans and expensive leather shoes. He is leaning against a rail outside of the restaurant speaking on his telephone. Earlier in the day at the carpark at Mount Rushmore we had seen a lot of large black bugs flying around. About an inch in length with legs and feet that hang noticeably from their bodies. Nickey has an irrational fear of anything that has more than four legs, add wings to that and it increases even further, almost to the point of bringing her to tears. She found them terrifying. Unbeknown to us, there are a whole load of these bugs on the wall of TGI Fridays just the other side of the rail on which this man is leaning. They are not unknown for too long, for as we walk past, we disturb them and they all take flight. A-brief-moment of chaos pursues. A swarm of almost biblical proportions, like locusts destroying everything in their path, fly around our heads. The fear that grips us would have any onlookers believe that these are huge, blood thirsty beasts with long, sharp fangs and claws that could lacerate the skin of a rhinoceros. The smart looking man on his telephone doesn't look quite so cool as he flaps his arms, dodging from side to side in a sheer panic, all the while trying to continue with his telephone conversation. Nickey, screaming and throwing her arms around, me, similar but without the screaming, begin to run to the entrance door. We dive in, fortunately there is a lobby area otherwise this would have been some entrance. We instantly try to regain our composure, brushing ourselves down we ask for a 'table for two please' as though nothing has happened.

As our heart rates return to the usual level, we laugh at ourselves and our over-reaction towards these harmless creatures. We have a drink and some lunch, sharing a platter as American football plays on television screens above our heads. We chat about the evening ahead and how much we are both looking forward to it. As we had an early start to the day, we are hopeful that we may get into our room soon to give us time for a short nap before heading back out. On leaving the restaurant to make our way back to our hotel we take a very wide birth of the wall that is home to the bugs, all the while keeping one eye firmly fixed on them in case we need to make another run for it.

We are handed our keys at about 2pm so are happy to have a bit of time to relax before the evening event.

Not long after getting into our room, Sarah, our tour operator, telephones us to firm up our arrangements for meeting prior to the Powwow. I tell her that we would need to eat before we meet and ask for any recommendations for our evening meal. Sarah suggests the Fire House in downtown Rapid City and agrees to meet us outside after we have eaten, at 6pm.

The Fire House is a pub/restaurant that not surprisingly has a fire rescue theme, with fire hydrants, firemen hats and hoses situated around the place. We have our meals, which are fine. Our waiter however, could be a bit friendlier, considering they rely so heavily on tips. When ordering our food, I make a little quip to which Nickey and I both laugh, our waiter's face remains straight, "I don't get British humour," he says. I comment on the word 'humour' being used loosely and we laugh again, well two of us do. Looks like a tough crowd tonight, I am paying him, he is relying on a tip, yet I still cannot get him to smile. His not so friendly demeaner is the complete opposite to other waiters and waitresses that I have encountered in the States. I hope that this job is just a stop gap for him, maybe to support himself through college, and that his chosen career path does not have him working with the general-public. I don't think it's for him. The tip I leave reflects his service.

We finish our meal and make our way outside just before six. Being five minutes early is being on-time right? As we have no idea what Sarah looks like, Nickey and I question each other quietly every time somebody approaches, "do you think this is her?" Time is ticking away, and our guessing game continues until about 6:30pm, becoming less fun with each minute that passes. With no telephone signal, we have no way of contacting to find out if all is ok, just like life pre-mobile phones. Just as we start to consider going on alone, a minibus pulls up, double parking as there are no free bays. A window rolls down and a female voice calls out, "Dave and Nickey?" We reply with a thankful, "yes". With this the side door slides open and out jumps a guy in a trilby style hat with a small feather in it. He is of a similar age to ourselves, and is carrying a hand-held drum along with a black case over his shoulder that I later found out contains a North American flute. This is our first meeting with Reuben FastHorse. After apologising for being late, explaining that they had been held up with a tour, he introduces himself, 'Reuben FastHorse', ensuring that we get the 'Reuben' part by likening it to a sandwich.

I have never heard of a Reuben sandwich but that is irrelevant, all I am thinking is, "What a cool name. Why can't I have a name like

Reuben FastHorse?" Not me, I am Dave Jones along with a billion others!

On our way back to the car, we make small talk the way you do when you meet somebody for the first time. Reuben tells us that he is a Lakota, from the Hunkpapa tribe and informs us of what we will be doing over the next two to three days, starting with this evenings Powwow.

We get into our car and drive the couple of blocks to where the Powwow is taking place. On this trip alone, I have already driven a fair few miles but for some reason on this short journey, my concentration levels seem to vanish and I start to drive as though it's my first time, almost forgetting which side of the road to drive on. Far too polite to say anything, Reuben sits there petrified, probably fearing for his life over the coming days. Nickey, on the other hand, certainly isn't so polite and makes sure that I'm aware of exactly what she thinks!!

Arriving safely at our destination, we all have a little laugh about it, although some more nervously than others.

Regarding the Powwow, I've had a bit of anxiety as to our behaviour, worried that Nickey or I may do something through ignorance that could offend. Before leaving England, I had looked online to find out do's and don'ts, checking on etiquette, here are some of the things that I read;

You should never call their regalia a costume.

Pointing with one finger is-seen-as rude and accusatory. You should point with your lips, head or chin, even with your hand but never a single finger.

You should not take photographs without permission.

If a feather falls from somebody's regalia, you should not touch it. You should make the person aware or inform one of the officials.

Do not sit in the seats close to the arena, they are reserved for participants and their families.

You must stand for the Grand Entrance.

There are more but you get the idea, it would be too easy to get something wrong.

We need not have worried. As far as I can make out, there are different-types of Powwows, some are intimate affairs and more family orientated, this one is open to all and therefore a little more relaxed, although, I might add that there are not many other white people here.

We pay our entrance fee and go on in. It is being held at the Rapid City civic centre which is a sports/concert arena and now also home to the city's ice hockey team that are playing this evening in another part of this large building. We have a wander around and look at the arts and craft stalls before making our way up to some of the elevated seats around the side. As we sit down, there's an awards ceremony taking place where Indians that have served in the military are being recognised and appreciated for their service along with a young girl being named 'Miss Lakota Nation', a title that she will hold for the following year. This award has been earned over the previous twelve months for services to her community along with achievements in education.

The most impressive part of the evening is the Grand Entrance, the main event of the weekend. The men, somewhere in the region of 100-200 of them, all dressed in full regalia enter the hall from the furthest corner to where we are sitting. Situated below us, there are six or seven guys sat around a large drum, they all beat in time with their single drumsticks. Along with the heavy beat, loud singing rings out from the same group, this accompanies the dancers as they enter the arena. They come out in a line maybe four or five deep as they follow one another, filtering into the hall in a spiral shape until the whole arena is full. Full of colour, full of movement and full of sound. I have seen Grand Entrances online before, but it's a completely different-experience seeing it live. The energy in the room is electric and the place feels like it's jumping. Goose bumps begin to form on the back of my neck and very quickly make their way down my arms. This is one of those moments where your body responds in a spontaneous way. There is no thought process, it is completely emotionally enthused. Visually it is spectacular, but it's way more than just something nice to watch, it triggers all of my senses and emotions in a way that happens very occasionally throughout our lives. As the performance comes to an end, Nickey and I look at each other and comment on how amazing it was, we both feel totally invigorated.

We hang around for a while, but nothing is going to top what we have just seen. We part company with Reuben for the evening, have one last walk around, buy an official t-shirt each and head back to our hotel for the night.

CHAPTER SIX

IN THE BEGINNING...

The following morning, we are still feeling the buzz from our experiences of last night's Grand Entrance. We have a coffee and a small breakfast before meeting Reuben in the reception of our hotel at 9:30 as arranged, ready to drive out and explore the Black Hills further.

A long day of driving ahead dictates our first stop of the day, the gas station. Nickey makes her way into the kiosk to pay as I add the fuel. When she returns to the car, she tells us that the man who served her was related to Sitting Bull. Reuben and I both laugh. "What?" Nickey asks. A direct descendant of Sitting Bull working in the gas station next to our hotel, how cool would that be...although incredibly unlikely!

I get the impression through speaking to Reuben that people claim many things, but the worst cases and most annoying to the Native Americans seem to be when white people say, "I have Native American blood. My grandmother was a Cherokee princess," or "I have Native American ancestors". They may laugh this off, but it's clearly an irritation to them. It appears that some non-Natives love to associate themselves with the romance of it, the living as one with nature, the proverbs, to the point of becoming a 'wannabe'. However, rarely do you see these people spending time on the reservations getting involved in the reality of being an Indian in modern day society. I'm very conscious of this and do my best to ensure that I don't project myself in this way. I make no claims of any such thing. It is important that I remain respectful to their culture throughout.

Under Reuben's guidance we head out of Rapid City and into the Black Hills. Within minutes we are pulling over to take some photographs of a bison that is walking along the roadside. There are open plains all around us and perfectly placed, some 50 feet away from the animal, there's a layby in which we park up. Close enough to take some pictures yet not too close to be considered dangerous. Just to be really safe, Nickey stays in the car. This beautiful creature walks towards us, it looks directly into our eyes. There are no distractions, just him and us. I'm curious as to why he's heading directly for us? Does he think we have food? Does he want to make friends? I'm not sure I want to find out. My heart beats a little faster with each step that brings him closer. Reuben and I stand just a few feet away from the car as I take a couple of photographs. I might have laughed at Nickey's lack of bravery but in my mind, I have a mark that, once he reaches it, I too am heading for the safety of our vehicle, "It's ok Reuben, I have enough pictures now thanks."

The bison is a huge beast. It instantly gives the impression of power and strength. To the Indians however, it represents so much more than just an impressive looking creature. To them it is a symbol of life. Throughout history it has been their main source of survival, to the point where, realising this the white man killed large numbers of this amazing animal as a deliberate attack on the Native Americans. Without this source of food and hide for warm clothing and shelter, life for the Indians would be a struggle.

Before we drive away from the layby, we also get a good look at some prairie dogs. They are cute looking creatures and although seen as a bit of a pest in these parts, we (especially Nickey) love watching them. They live in large numbers and an area that's home to a group of them is called a town. As we watch on, they stand on their hind legs keeping lookout in a similar way to meerkats and bark, which is a short exclamation, similar to a human trying to clear their throat with a dry, sharp cough. Seeing wildlife may not be the main-focus of our trip, however, most people love to see animals that they've not seen before and we are no exception.

Our first real place of interest for the day is to be Wind Cave. A lot of Lakota people believe that the first of their tribe to walk the earth came out of this cave, others believe they come from the stars. As we drive towards the cave, I mention how dark it must be out here at night, with no un-natural light it must be quite spectacular looking up at the pitch-black sky with just the illuminations of the moon and planets. Reuben nods in agreement. This prompts him to tell us of a belief that some Lakota people have. They believe that when they die, their spirit goes up to the stars, they walk along the Milky Way, on reaching the fork, a wise old lady is waiting for them. She questions them on their life. If they have not been a good person, they walk the short prong, falling back down to Earth to live another, hopefully better life. No Hell. No eternal condemnation, just an opportunity to put things right.

At Wind Cave, as we walk from the car to the visitor's centre, we see a very small snake, the size of a slow worm that can commonly be seen in long grass and woodlands in the U.K. Reuben catches it and assures us that it's a garter snake and not poisonous, so I hold it for a few moments. I don't have a fear of snakes, however, I certainly respect the fact that a lot of them could kill me! Thankfully not this one though. I've held snakes in the past, we had a pair of royal pythons as family pets when I was younger. Contrary to what some believe, they are not slimy, smooth is a much better description. I let this little fella move freely between my fingers, passing it from one hand to the other before gently placing it back on the ground to continue with its journey.

After taking a short walk around the visitors centre and reading some information boards that explain how the caves are formed beneath our feet, Reuben leads us along a dirt track overhung with trees. The sunlight breaks through the gaps in the branches, creating shadows on the path in front of us. Within a few moments we reach the spot from where it is believed the Lakota people came. I was expecting a big entrance with far more hype surrounding it, this is America after all. This highlights how far more reserved the Indians are compared to the rest of the people in the United States. It's just a small opening. There's no big fuss, no flags nor bunting. No fireworks nor parades. Just a hole in the ground with a small wall around it and an information board which reads;

'This place gave birth to a nation. Native Nations have recognized this special place since time immemorial. The Lakota Nation, in particular, chronicles this opening as the place of emergence of their people, "Pte Oyate" – buffalo nation, to the surface of the world. Their creation story says they were beneath the surface and were led to the sunlight by Tokahe (the first to come). The cave represents the buffalo's interior complete with organs, meat, and medicines. After emergence, the Lakota saw the Black Hills were in the shape of a buffalo lying down and facing east, solidifying the relationship with Pte Oyate that still exists. Afterwards, they assembled a holistic view termed "Wolakota"- natural law encompassing all that exists, that includes all places viewed as sacred. This is one of many sacred places of Native people and it is treated with respect at all times. mitakuye oyasin'

I love the phrase 'mitakuye oyasin'. Seen by some as a prayer which translated literally means - we are all related, we are all connected within the universe.

We walk on a little further down the dirt track, it is peaceful, there is nobody else in this area. The quiet is warming, no people means no distractions, our full attention is fixed on where we are and the subject of the Lakota nation. A clearing in the trees with some picnic tables makes an ideal place to stop and chat for a while. Reuben plays his drum and sings a traditional Lakota song, followed by a tune on the North American flute (he tends to carry these instruments with him on a regular basis). He speaks about the Lakota language and that only 2% of Lakota people now speak it, the average age of which is 65 years old. They are trying to re-introduce it to the young so that it doesn't fade away. When Reuben speaks in his native tongue it captivates me. I love the way it flows. It sounds so calm, almost hypnotic. Each word rolls into the next with a poetic fluidity. I hope they are successful in keeping it alive, after all it is a major player in Lakota people remaining Lakota.

We leave Wind Cave and head further into the hills. Our next destination is the Crazy Horse memorial, a place that also has some controversy surrounding it. This isn't necessarily the sort of place that is on our 'must see' list, more of a tourist attraction than something of significance but because of the contentious views on it, I would like to visit.

On our way there we stop for some lunch in a town called Custer. With it being a Sunday on a holiday weekend, many of the places are closed, but as is the case the whole-world over, fast food restaurants are always an option. Today this may seem like a good thing, without them we would go hungry, but strip back to the reason why we are here, and you question whether life is better with them? With a handful of these large chains having the monopoly on this industry, it could not be any further from the true ethics of the Native Americans that strongly believe in sharing and helping each other. People do not go hungry whilst others feast in the Lakota community. On a more personal note, the sad thing about this is that these places are the same the world over too. We could be sat in our home town eating the same thing, with the same layout, same décor and so on. We refuel our bodies yet add nothing to our experiences in the way Emporium had. Our options on this occasion are limited and therefore it's pizza for lunch.

A couple of doors up from the pizza restaurant there is a gift shop that sells Native American souvenirs. Nickey wants to buy some moccasins so we stop to see what they have to offer. We purchase a pair along with a small drum with a picture of an eagle and feathers hanging from it for our granddaughter. There are certain things that are a bit 'cliché', such as buying dreamcatchers, drums and moccasins but it is a trap that we willingly fall into. We are also guilty of similar when visiting India, like many others we buy models of elephants and Hindu Gods! I like to see it as doing our bit to help with the tourism trade. In both of these places, our money is needed to aid the living expenses of the people selling.

We return once again to the car and Reuben informs me that we need to head in the opposite direction to which we are facing. The beauty of American roads is that they're very wide, a u-turn can be done in one swift manoeuvre, especially today as there's not much traffic. So, that's what I do. "Did you not see that sheriff's car?" Reuben laughs nervously as he asks. The truth is, no I didn't but even if I had I would've done it anyway, totally oblivious to the fact that it was not allowed. Apparently, there were solid lines in the centre of the road which means no u-turns. Realising that I was obviously a tourist and more trouble than he needed on such a peaceful Sunday, the police officer looks at me, looks at Reuben, then continues with his day. I think I would have done the same.

If Sitting Bull was the great spiritual leader and medicine man of the Lakota people, then Crazy Horse was the great warrior. Together they were a formidable pair. Crazy Horse proved himself time and again to be fearless in battle, most famously at the Fetterman Fight and the Little Big Horn. We will be visiting these battlefields later on our journey.

The Crazy Horse memorial sits high in the rock face and can be seen from miles around. We first caught a glimpse of it as we drove from Torrington to Mount Rushmore the previous day. It is a large engraving, in a similar fashion to that of the four Presidents heads. Still a long way from being finished, we get to see how it will look on completion (if that ever happens) from models that they have on show. It sits just a couple of miles from Mount Rushmore, I assume in order of balance. So, why would some people not be happy to have this?

Some believe that rock faces should just be left in their natural state, in which case there's no place for either of these monuments. Some of the Lakota people aren't happy because, when finished, Crazy Horse will be pointing with one finger out over the local area, focusing on his quote, "My lands are where my dead lie buried". As we know, pointing with one finger is not acceptable.

Apparently, there are no authenticated pictures of Crazy Horse. He was an unassuming man and unlikely to have had his photograph taken. The image that they have been working towards has been created by descriptions being passed through the generations.

With a lot of people not keen on its existence, who decided on putting it here in the first place? I wrongly believed, before my trip, that it was a gesture of the American Government. It was not and has had no Government funding. There is an entrance fee, although as we are with Reuben (Lakota people along with their guests gain free entry) we do not contribute. This money goes towards the continuation of the work that will one day hopefully see its completion.

It was Chief Henry Standing Bear with support of other chiefs that wanted this memorial, "My fellow chiefs and I would like the white man to know that the red man has great heroes, too," his reasoning for the project. Polish/American sculptor Korczak Ziolkowski was approached to undertake the task of creating the memorial.

In the impressive visitor's centre located close to the rock face, we watch a video showing how the sculpture has got to its current form, mostly through dynamite, and how Korczak Ziolkowski dedicated his life to this. Sadly, he is no longer with us and the baton has been passed on to his family.

I wasn't sure of my view regarding the memorial, yet as I write I find myself swinging to the side of it being a good thing. With the reason behind it being a genuine one, I find it hard to condemn. Others may disagree. Reuben remains professional and stays neutral with his view.

From the memorial we take the scenic route back to Rapid City. Winding roads through wooded hills with some interesting rock formations along the sides, some of which have created tunnels that you drive through. They stand in different shapes and sizes, some sandy in colour, some grey. Some with jutted edges, some smooth, no two are the same.

We stop for one last time at a place called Sylvan Lake, also known as the Crown Jewel of Custer National Park. When you add water to an already beautiful landscape, it always seems to enhance it even further. With more of these rocks raising up out of the ground sporadically in and at the edge of the lake, you can easily see where it gets its nickname.

We enjoy a walk around the water's edge and take some photographs. There is a wedding ceremony taking place in a small opening close to the lake and for some reason I snap a picture of the bride and groom too. I have no idea why as they are complete strangers to me, but at this moment it seems like the right thing to do. What is such an important day for this couple in a beautiful setting, draws me into the moment. I hope, in years to come, their day will remain as memorable to them as mine has been to me.

The wind picks up and the temperature drops, it turns from a comfortable cool to an uncomfortable chill. This dictates how long we spend here, shortening it from what we would have liked. We reluctantly leave this beautiful spot and head for home.

Back in Rapid City, we drop Reuben at his house, grab a bite to eat at a buffet style restaurant, then make our way back to our hotel for the night.

We have already seen so much on this trip. Every day brings an anticipation of more excitement. What more could tomorrow possibly bring?

CHAPTER SEVEN

RED CLOUD

No longer do I feel like a tourist outside looking in but more engulfed by the whole thing. I challenge anyone with an ounce of compassion to stand where we stood at Wounded Knee without being at least a little affected. Maybe not to the extent that I have, yet affected nonetheless.

It's Christopher Columbus Day and we pick Reuben up from his home just after 9:30am (making our own time arrangements was one of the benefits of having a personal guide). Today we will be visiting Pine Ridge and driving through the Badlands.

Once again, we head out of Rapid City and into the wide-open plains. The more time we spend in these surroundings the more at home I feel, becoming totally relaxed within them as well as the company that I'm in. By now we have become good friends with Reuben and as we drive he asks us about English comedy. He mentions some of the comedians from the past such as Benny Hill and Monty Python. I mention Ricky Gervais as he is one of my favourite comedians, Reuben has heard of him. I also put him onto some modern day stand-up comics that he hasn't heard of, the likes of Mickey Flanagan and Peter Kay, explaining how they are from different-parts of the country and therefore have completely different accents. By that evening he was posting YouTube clips of both these men on social media. Benny Hill and Monty Python? We have moved on a bit since then.

Not too far into our drive Reuben prompts me to pull over onto the grass verge by the side of the road. He points to a small tree that stands alone in a field, it has prayer ties hanging from it. A bit further on beyond the tree there's a barn. Reuben explains that this area is the setting for a Sundance.

Sundances are spiritual ceremonies and the highest form of worship within the Native American culture. They take place once a year, usually in the height of summer. The Indians believe in suffering for their prayers so endure 4 days in the heat with no food nor water. The men wear nothing but a skirt and the women just a cloth dress as they dance barefoot. In the past it was predominantly males that would partake but in modern times women have joined them. Participants can volunteer to dance for themselves or for somebody in need, for example a sick family member or friend.

The tree is picked by the dance leader or chief, a virgin makes the first chop and it is carried to the site of the dance without touching the ground until it reaches the 'arbor', the place that has been prepared for its arrival. This is where it will sit until the following year when it will be replaced by the next one.

Once in its position, the tree is decorated with cut out rawhide images of a man, the sun, the moon, stars, a woman and a bison.

To me, giving up food and water for four whole days whilst dancing in the summer heat sounds like a huge sacrifice, however, a lot of the Indian men go even further by piercing the skin in the pectoral area, hooking to the tree and then breaking from it. Some may even drag six buffalo skulls hooked into their backs as they dance around the arbor. At the end of the four days some of the women will pierce the tops of their arms in the deltoid area too. All of these sacrifices are made for the benefit of their dreams, visions or prayers.

The ceremony ends when a virgin, representing the goddess of the White Buffalo Calf Woman, wearing four shawls walks towards the east shedding one shawl at a time.

Before continuing with our drive, to take this in, I pause for a few moments. I want to digest what I have just heard. That is a serious dedication to what you believe. From the high levels of discomfort brought on by hunger and thirst, to the extreme pain of the physical actions that they carry out on their own bodies, the mental focus is immense. It shows just how far we can push our pain threshold when we have a complete will to do so. Although, I am not so sure I have the inner strength to do it myself. As I pull away from the grass verge, I do so with images of men with hooks in their backs dragging buffalo skulls going through my mind.

A little further on and Reuben signals for me to stop once more. We have now reached the edge of the Badlands, named as such because it is very barren and not good for agriculture and livestock. We step away from the car and look down from an elevated position across a sea of rocks and clay, raising up from the ground in random formations across a large valley. In the same way that I could sit and look at the ocean or into a fire for long-periods, I could sit looking at this. It may not be a place for things to flourish but it is mesmerizing to look at and a wondrous natural spectacle.

Entering Pine Ridge, we start to pass groups of residential dwellings, these are called 'clusters'. Within the clusters there are a number of properties, many of which have old cars that have long since been used as modes of transport, sat in the yard. These tend now to be used for extra storage space as room in the homes is limited. I am surprised that there are no small convenience stores among the clusters but there are not. I can't help but think there could be an opportunity for somebody here.

Our plan is to visit Red Cloud School on our way through, however, as this day is a public holiday the school is closed. This does not prevent us from going but it means that we cannot go inside, our visit is restricted. Reuben attempts to open one of the entrance doors in the hope that there maybe somebody around, but it's locked. There's a church/chapel just across the carpark, this is open, the 'house of God' is never closed I guess. We go in, there's nobody here either. Schools without children are quiet places. As they are usually full of activity, when they are empty they feel a little soulless. Without anybody here to speak to, we decide to take a walk around the grounds of the school. Reuben points out some living accommodation that is residence to some of the staff that work here. Newly qualified teachers from out of town frequently come here to learn their trade. If the teachers are successful, they tend to move on. However, some do fall in love with the place and stay.

Reuben leads us up a hill to a cemetery. This is the resting place of Red Cloud. A few precious moments are spent at his grave.

Red Cloud was a leader of the Oglala people at the same time as Sitting Bull was a Hunkpapa chief and Crazy Horse an Oglala warrior. They never always saw eye to eye as Red Cloud agreed to the treaties and Sitting Bull did not.

In his earlier years Red Cloud was up for the fight against the whites and played a major part in the battles that took place along the Bozeman Trail. It is believed however, that after a visit to Washington DC, where he saw the huge volume of people that lived in the cities he realised that the Indians were fighting a losing battle. For every white soldier killed there was another ready to take his place, for every Indian warrior killed it would take 14 years to replace them.

Sitting Bull and Crazy Horse, among others, believed that Red Cloud had become weak, no longer having the stomach for the struggle in the same way they had.

Reuben tells us that, as a child, he had attended this school. We're disappointed that we cannot take a better look. When I return I shall visit again.

We never spent a whole lot of time at Pine Ridge and I never realised how much it, along with our visit to Wounded Knee, had affected me until I arrived back in England. As I have only seen a small portion of it, and also looked up some statistics that I have written about in an earlier chapter, I'm looking forward to returning to dig a little deeper, not just to Pine Ridge but in general. My flight is now booked, and I am counting down the days to when I see Reuben again and spend some more time exploring.

Not many people visit Pine Ridge, Reuben informs us that he rarely brings tours here. Its reputation has people fearing for what they may experience should they come. I can only say that we have had no problems. At the places that we stop and interact with the locals, such as the gas station and a restaurant on our way out from Wounded Knee, we are treated in the same way that we have been treated everywhere else, with politeness and courtesy (with maybe the exception of our waiter with no sense of humour in Rapid City). Maybe the fact that we are with Reuben and less likely to take a wrong turn helps. I have no idea what to expect from my next trip, but I have no fears.

We visit Wounded Knee then make our way off-of the reservation. Our journey back would have us drive right through the Badlands, not the part that we had seen earlier but a large section right through the heart of it. It feels as though we have just driven onto the set of a western movie. The road is surrounded by very tall rocks for as far as our eyes can see. As we drive on through the quiet, winding road, in my mind I swap my car for a horse and the tarmac road for a dirt track. For a few short moments, my imagination has me back in the 1800's riding through this desolate land. I picture myself chewing tobacco as I sit with my hands holding the reins loosely, resting them on the top of my saddle. The horse walks slowly as I spit out the tobacco onto the dusty path. In truth, I could not think of anything worse than putting chewing tobacco in my mouth, but hey, it looks cool and that's all that matters in this little fantasy that I'm living out in my head.

The road takes us up a hill where there are parking areas at regular intervals. We come across another elevated bay, we make use of this opportunity to take in this surreal scenery, getting out of our car and walking to the edge of the rock face (this is the photograph on the front cover). I'm not keen on heights, actually-that's an understatement, I am petrified of heights and our position has us looking out from the edge with a severe drop just a few feet in front of us. I sit on the ground, for some reason this helps with the vertigo. I ask Reuben if he would mind me playing his drum and he allows me to do so. I beat out a steady rhythm as Reuben sings a song in his Lakota language which, when translated means, 'My people, the good that you see is me. Whenever I walk on this road of life I try to think positive', I feel a part of the whole experience, a special moment.

The light is beginning to fade as we make our way out of the Badlands and head back to Rapid City. It has been a long day and a very significant one in relation to my journey.

Tonight's drive back is tinged with sadness for this is to be our last day with Reuben FastHorse. Some people that we meet in our lives become instant friends, you seem to click as though you have known each other for years. This is the case with Reuben and ourselves. We drop him back at his home and say our goodbyes. We hug, and you can feel that the bond is strong. Something inside of me knew that this was not the last time we would cross paths. I'm glad that it was not, for over time, Reuben has become like a Lakota brother to me. Good bye my friend, for now at least.

CHAPTER EIGHT

BEAR BUTTE AND DEVILS TOWER

Good bye Rapid City, time to move on. Today we drive out of South Dakota and head back into Wyoming, our destination, a town called Sheridan. We will not be going directly there however, as we have plans to go via Bear Butte and Devils Tower. We get onto the highway and head out of town. Big billboards signal the exit for Deadwood, Calamity Jane country. We are a little tempted to pull off and explore, but with two stops already scheduled we think it is best that we push on.

On we go to Bear Butte, driving through the town of Sturgis as we get closer to the mountain. You may remember Sturgis being mentioned by the couple at Emporium. It is host to a big biker rally each year. It certainly has the feel of a biker's town with the style of bars by the roadside. As we drive we see a large sculpture mounted on a post, it sits some twenty feet high and is of a flaming biker made from scrap metal. It looks like the Grim Reaper riding a chopper with flames trailing behind in the wind. It holds in one hand, a chainsaw. It is impressive, albeit a little intimidating. This stands outside of the

Full Throttle Saloon. The bars look like modern versions of saloons from the days of the old wild west. As it's still quite early, there are not many people about, yet there is no escaping the fact that this is Sturgis, home of one of the world's largest biker rallies.

We drive through the town and out the other side, in the distance Bear Butte stands before us. We make our way towards it and reach a campsite set by the side of a lake where we stop for a short while. It is quiet, yet very windy.

Bear Butte stands 1,349m above sea level and is seen as a sacred mountain by the Indians. Many still take pilgrimages here and leave prayer ties and tobacco bundles hanging from the branches of trees. It's a place where Indians have travelled for meditation and prayers for hundreds of years. It gets its name because if you look from a certain side it resembles a bear lying down.

We are not sure if there is an information centre here, (I have since discovered that there is). We decide not to spend time looking and take our viewpoint from the lakeside. I would estimate that we are approximately half a mile from the mountain, between us, just open grassland. Other than the occasional passing vehicle, we are alone. The wind is very strong as seems to be common in South Dakota. It is loud as it blows around our heads. The solitude and the feeling of being at one with nature, along with the difficult elements, make this a perfect setting for the pilgrims that have been drawn here for many, many years. For the more tuned in, I'm sure the wind can be heard as a voice. The voice of the creator. The message? That's for each-individual to interpret in their own way.

Bear Butte is more about its spiritual significance than how it looks as part of the landscape. Although it is nice to look at, there are places of greater beauty around the world. Do they share the same importance as Bear Butte to the people? That's a whole other question.

Having read other people's accounts of their trips to Bear Butte and their overwhelming feel of emotion, it leaves me with one regret, that we never actually climbed the mountain. The amount of regrets that I have from my trips can be counted on one hand, yet maybe this is one that will need to be addressed at a later date. Reuben, get your walking boots out.

For now, and as far as this trip goes, we leave Bear Butte. Next stop Devils Tower.

A lot of time is spent on the road today. From the time we leave Rapid City to when we reach Sheridan is between six and seven hours. The section from Bear Butte to Devils Tower does not take too long, however, once the Tower comes into view, it takes what seems like an eternity to get there. Not because of anything such as monotony, more because we're both in desperate need of a bathroom. Considering the number of miles that we travel, it's amazing that this is the only time I can recall this happening.

Eventually we reach the edge of the park at which Devils Tower stands, an impressive rock that raises out of the ground, standing 1,559m from sea level. It can be seen for miles around, your eyes are drawn to it because it sits apart from the rest of the landscape, standing alone in an otherwise relatively flat area. We arrive at the park, first things first, fortunately, there are some gift shops with cafes attached but most importantly, toilets.

Just beyond the shops sits a booth where you pay your entrance fee before slowly driving up a winding road to the visitor's centre and parking area. Either side of the entrance booth offers a great photo opportunity, the best position to get a shot with both myself and Devils Tower sat behind me. This is also a good place to get yet more pictures of prairie dogs, there are many here. This pleases Nickey, she has become quite obsessed with them.

Most people recognise Devils Tower from the movie 'Close Encounters of The Third Kind' or more recently a lesser known film called 'Paul', a light-hearted comedy about two English guys travelling there in a camper van that pick up an alien en route.

We drive up at a steady incline to reach the foot of the actual tower.

Some come here to climb the rock yet most, like us, just to take-a-look. It stands, a rectangular shape with a flat top. All around the sides there are deep vertical grooves that go from top to bottom. There are a few legendary stories regarding Devils Tower, this being my favourite...

The Lakota people believe that seven girls were out playing when they were chased by a bear. As the bear closed in on them they stood on a rock and prayed to the Great Spirit to help them. With this the rock rose up out of the ground and the girls became unreachable. The grooves in the sides of the rock are from the claws of the angry bear as it tried in vain to reach them. It is believed that the rock continued to rise and took the girls up to the heavens where they became stars. The star formation Pleiades that can be seen above the rock at night, according to this legendary story, is the girls looking down.

The bear, after failing in its attempts to reach the girls left Devils Tower, travelled for some distance before laying down to rest. This is where it went into hibernation, lying on its side facing east. This is believed to be Bear Butte.

I love these legendary stories that are passed down through the generations. Experiencing other cultures and beliefs are what make travelling such a wonderful thing

Having seen the two things on our list for the day, we continue on to Sheridan.

Most of our journey is on a fast road. Within no time we are bombing along at 80mph.

There's no doubt about it, road trips are great adventures, however, travelling long distances in America can throw up the odd problem, well one in particular. The roads go on forever and you are not sure how far you will travel before you come across the next fuelling station. This journey has me worrying a little that we may run out of gas. As the fuel gauge registers less than a quarter of a tank, my eyes are constantly being drawn towards it and with each mile that passes without any sign of a gas station the concern grows a tad stronger. When in unfamiliar surroundings it's easy to become a little irrational about things. It's a little early to panic but what if we run out? What will I do? I thought it best not to mention it to Nickey, her being aware would in no way improve the situation.

Fortunately, with the needle hovering just above the red, we see a sign for a service station. We pull off the main road, drive a quarter of a mile or so and there it is, our saviour. Maybe if it were dark, Pleiades would be shining bright above this gas station with the seven girls guiding us through our difficult moment. Not quite as daunting as being chased by a bear I admit, but in our molly coddled society, with all of the instant gratification that we demand, this was fast becoming an issue. We fill up. Right to the very top. Panic over.

I take this as a lesson learned and make sure that I fill up at more regular intervals.

Now relaxed, we carry on with the final stretch of today's drive.

We travel many miles through open plains, in the far distance mountains surround us. This is the area between the Black Hills and The Little Big Horn that was given to the Natives as hunting ground in the treaty of 1868. Whichever direction our eyes look, the scenery is equally beautiful. Eventually we reach the exit for Sheridan and leave the highway. Our hotel is just a couple of minutes away. It is nice to arrive at our destination, the next place that we shall be calling home, even if it is just for a few days.

Across the road from the front of our hotel, beyond a patch of grass, there is a large Wal-Mart. Beside the supermarket is a Burger King, next to which is a Perkins, another restaurant from a large chain. Everything that we could possibly need within walking distance. With a lot of hours behind the wheel, it has been a tiring day. A burger and an early night sees a close to another chapter of our journey.

CHAPTER NINE

FETTERMAN FIGHT

A new day, a new town, a new guide.

Over the coming days we shall be visiting some of the famous battle sites from the 1800's such as The Fetterman Fight, The Battle of The Rosebud, and of course, The Battle of The Little Big Horn also known as Custer's Last Stand.

When we booked this trip, these were at the top of the list of things that I wanted to see yet having experienced what we already have, they have become just an extension of the amazing journey that we have found ourselves on.

Our first morning in Sheridan is a free one, we are not meeting our next guide until early afternoon so have a little spare time to explore this small town. We take a short drive from our hotel to the main street (not sure if it is called 'Main Street' but it's highly likely that it is). All of the towns that we visit tend to have a street such as this, which is lined with shops, the odd restaurant/café, a bank, an estate-agents etc. These streets feel very American and there's no mistaking that we are deep in the mid-west of the country. It's not out of place to see men in cowboy hats, wearing Wrangler jeans and boots.

We park at the side of the road and take a leisurely stroll along. We go into a shoe shop and buy another pair of moccasins, this time for our granddaughter. We wander around a shop that sells bric-a-brac and look in the windows of others, some selling clothes others selling paintings and so on. Once we have walked from one end of the street to the other, we return to our hotel, park the car and walk over to Perkins to have some lunch ready for meeting with our new guide, Rose Williams, and our afternoon excursion.

As it is a nice sunny day, we are sat outside when Rose arrives. She's a smartly dressed woman, wearing a black blazer with a beige shirt and colourful tie. Rose also wears dark denim jeans and leather boots. On her head she has a cream coloured hat that resembles a cross between a sun hat and a cowboy hat, her braided hair hangs from it over her shoulders. I later find out that this is a Crow hat, as in worn by members of the Crow tribe. We find out over the coming days that Rose is very much a Crow, by that I mean she is extremely proud of her heritage, and although very neutral in her teaching, there certainly is no hiding this fact. We love this about her and the fact that she remains true to who she is.

Our first trip with Rose is a visit to Fort Phil Kearney on the Bozeman Trail, the battle site of the Fetterman Fight. This is not too far from Sheridan. After introducing ourselves, we jump into the car and make our way there.

Rose is initially more formal than Reuben but after being with us for a while she becomes more relaxed and we enjoy our time with her.

As we drive towards the Fort, Rose explains how the Crows and Lakotas have been enemies for hundreds of years. The Crows never fought against the whites, instead acted as scouts for them. The reason they chose not to fight, Rose tells us, is because of a dream had by a young boy in which he saw many trees in a forest, after a strong wind came, all of the trees were blown down...except one. It did not suffer the same fate as the others, it is believed, because it leant in the same direction the wind was blowing. The interpretation of the Crow people was that the wind represented the Government, the trees that fell were the other tribes and the one that remained standing was the Crows. So, they made the decision to go with the Government rather than against them.

At this point, I realise that I seem to have already formed a bit of an allegiance to the Lakota people, partly through spending time with Reuben and partly because of the things that I have read and seen. I love this story that Rose has just told us, however, I feel disappointed that the Crows chose this course of action. I don't share this with Rose, it would be disrespectful and somewhat inappropriate. It's not my position to judge and as I'm not, nor have ever been directly affected by any of this, I suppress my feelings, attempting to store this knowledge in an unbiased way. I do wonder if, with the beauty of hindsight, they would have done things differently.

We drive into the carpark at Fort Phil Kearney. Once again, there are not many other cars around. I get the impression that Americans are not largely into their history (well this side of it anyway), I mention this to Rose and she confirms what I already know regarding the history taught in schools is a little distorted. I tell her, as I understand it, this subject is touched upon briefly in schools in the UK nowadays. This may increase the interest in the future with UK visitors at least. Other than our visit to the Little Big Horn, the lack of interest in these places seems to be common.

We walk into the visitor's centre and are greeted by the lady that works here. Two men dressed in camouflage clothing that are about to go hunting (I assume for prairie dogs...I don't share my thoughts with Nickey) follow us in, buy some permits and leave. Nickey and I watch a short video which relays the story of this battle to us. Once the film has finished, the lady, along with Rose elaborates on what we have just learned.

The Fetterman Fight is also known to many as the Fetterman Massacre, or to the Indians as Red Cloud's War. I have chosen the word 'fight' rather than 'massacre' after speaking to a historian that is a good friend of Reubens', Dakota GoodHouse. Dakota has been kind enough to give me the occasional piece of advice here and there throughout my journey. When he sees that I've used the word 'massacre', he questions whether this could be a bit misleading. After all it was a battle between armed soldiers and warriors. It was a massacre in the sense of a heavy defeat yet not a massacre in the same way as Wounded Knee for example. I fully agree with Dakota and have opted to use the word 'fight'. I assume they chose 'fight' over 'battle' with alliteration in mind.

48

This is the first battle site of three that we visit. I have heard of all of these battles, but my knowledge is limited. If you are in the same position, then I hope that over the coming two to three chapters things will be a little clearer as to what happened and how they occurred with relation to one another. The aim is to, within the context of my journey, give a brief-summary of how things unfolded during this period. There are many text books that go into greater detail, however, if you are like me, reading these books can be a little daunting. Hopefully this will give you a decent enough foundation. There are also different versions of events depending on whom you speak to or what you read, I can only give my interpretation of what I've been told, how I see it.

The Bozeman Trail connected the gold rush area of Montana to the Oregon Trail. As this became increasingly busier with traffic, the Indians became more and more angered by the travellers moving through their lands and scaring away the buffalo, their main source of survival. They began to attack the wagons as they passed through in the hope that it would deter others. Instead, in 1866 the Government decided that they would place three forts along the trail to protect the travellers. A counsel was held with the Indians regarding this, leading them to believe that they had a say on the outcome. It became apparent that their opinions were irrelevant when, during the counsel, with the worst possible timing, Colonel Carrington and his men marched into view with the obvious intention of starting work on the forts. This caused uproar with Red Cloud, who was the leading Oglala chief at the time, along with other chiefs present and the counsel came to an abrupt end.

Within just a few months a complete fort was built, Fort Phil Kearney. Relations with the Indians were now strained, and skirmishes were occurring on a regular basis. On December 21st of 1866 hostilities reached boiling point and the Fetterman Fight took place four miles outside of the fort.

When a wood train (a group out collecting wood to supply the fort) came under Indian attack, assistance was called for. Fetterman was sent to give support, accompanied by 80 men consisting of officers, cavalry and infantry. Despite firm warnings from Carrington not to pursue the enemy beyond Lodge Ridge Trail, they did so and marched straight into an ambush. This is where Crazy Horse really began to make a name for himself as a great warrior. He was instrumental in drawing the soldiers out to where his men lay in waiting.

Having personally stood in the very spot where the battle took place, I can only imagine the fear that must have gripped the soldiers. After being led onto the ridge, their enemy could come at them from either side, not being visible until they were right on top of them. There really was no way of escape. With single shot muskets as their main source of protection, a weapon with a very slow reloading process, Fetterman's men were little more than sitting ducks. Indians came at them from every direction and the outcome of zero survivors was inevitable.

A very well thought out plan and one of the heaviest defeats suffered by the whites at the hands of the Indians at that time.

Over the next two years more skirmishes took place until in 1868 the Government conceded defeat and evacuated the forts, leaving them empty. These were destroyed by the Indians.

Obviously with the forts being demolished the buildings are no longer here. However, the perimeter has been marked out and a replica fence put in place so that you can stand behind it and look out at the surroundings in the same way the occupants would have. The Fort sits at the foot of a number of grass covered hills. You cannot see beyond them, so have no idea what or whom lays behind. Strangely, prior to the Fetterman Fight, the people that lived here were not scared of the Indians as up until this point, they never saw them as a major threat. They saw them as weak, clearly they underestimated their opposition. Today, on top of these hills in the distance stands cut out Indians on horseback. This gives a good feel of what would have been seen between 1866 and 1868 when hostilities were at their worst. It appears that the warning signs were there, just not heeded.

We leave the fort late afternoon and drive back to Sheridan. We arrange a time and place to meet Rose the following morning and ask what she has planned for the evening. Rose has children ranging from very young to late teens. This obviously takes up most of her time, but she also tells us that she loves going to the casino and would do so if she ever got a spare hour. This was her way of winding down.

Our evening would consist of laying on our hotel bed watching television until we fall asleep full of contentment.

CHAPTER TEN

DEER MEDICINE ROCK AND THE BATTLE OF THE ROSEBUD

The great-thing with this part of the world is that you can work out how long it will take you to get from one place to another by knowing the distance and the speed at which you will be travelling. This seems like a simple equation that should be the same wherever you are but we all know this is not the case because of the unpredictability of traffic.

The journey from Sheridan to the Trading Post, where we have arranged to meet Rose, takes an hour. In England we use the term, "on a good run", here, every run is a "good run". This is something that the local people take for granted but for us, it's very novel. We will be driving this same route daily for the next three days.

The hour drive sees us enter Montana. Well, there cannot be many commutes that are as enjoyable as this one. We watch the white-tailed deer run in small herds in the open grassland that our highway passes through, mountains perfectly situated as a distant back drop like a beautiful painting. We have become a little blasé about the beauty that surrounds us, even to the point of expecting it, but I would not swap it for any other.

The Trading Post is a large log cabin set back from the road. As we approach it, we see four coloured tipis that line the front of the carpark along the roadside. The wooden building stands alone, another white tipi is erected just to the side of the entrance, this one is for sale. We make our way inside, it is set up as a café to the left, you can smell the coffee as you walk in, the rest is a shop that sells Native American goods and souvenirs. Native American singing fills the room, piped through speakers, a song which I have since become familiar with is playing. Every time I hear it now, my mind takes me back to the Trading Post and these very special days. Situated in close proximity to the site of the Battle of The Little Big Horn and not too far from the location of the Battle of The Rosebud makes this the ideal place to meet Rose.

According to my itinerary, on this day we are set to visit Deer Medicine Rock along with the Battle of The Rosebud site. Deer Medicine Rock is where Sitting Bull, during a Sundance, had his vision of soldiers falling head first into the Indian camp. This gave his people great belief that a big victory was heading their way. Two weeks later they defeated Custer at the Battle of The Little Big Horn. Sitting Bull etched engravings into the rock, these are still visible today. As a person that has a huge respect for this great chief, to the point of having a large portrait of him tattooed on my chest, I'm very keen to see this.

Nickey and I are sat outside of the Trading Post drinking coffee when Rose arrives. We greet each other with the usual "good morning, hope you had a nice evening", before making our way to our vehicle and climbing in. As we settle into our seats I mention that, based on my paperwork, today will have us going to Deer Medicine Rock and the Rosebud battlefield. Rose's face drops, and her expression becomes one of fearful displeasure, "Deer Medicine Rock could be a problem. It can be dangerous up there," she says.

As I start to wonder what sort of danger she means, (could it be a dangerous climb? I don't know) Rose continues, "and I haven't smudged this morning." Still not totally understanding the problem but realising that it's pretty-serious stuff to Rose, I offer not to go.

She goes on to explain that she knows of three people that have died within a year of going up there and that if we are to go we will have to be very respectful and would most certainly need to smudge, this is a spiritual ritual carried out regularly by Native Americans, although at this point, something that Nickey and I had never partaken in. With this, Rose climbs out of the car and heads back into the Trading Post. She returns a couple of minutes later with some lemon grass that had been braided into a rectangular shape. This will be used for us to smudge with before we go up to the rock.

Sitting Bull, during the Sundance had called upon the Great Spirit, to inflict bad things on his enemies. "Is it because you are a Crow?" I ask naively. "And you are white people," Rose replies. On hearing this I become very interested to know what I need to do to smudge before we go there. I have never really seen myself as spiritual, however when you are surrounded by people that are, your attitude changes. Rose is incredibly spiritual.

Before we go to Deer Medicine Rock we will first be visiting the Rosebud battleground. As we drive, Rose picks up the story from the Fetterman Fight and the 1868 evacuation from the forts on the Bozeman Trail...

After 1868 there was a period of relative calm. The treaty had been signed and the Lakota people were left to live peacefully in the Black Hills, until gold was discovered there. At the end of 1875, after a failed attempt by the Government to buy the Black Hills (the Indians to this day have never accepted payment for this sacred land, as far as they are concerned, the Black Hills are not for sale and never have been), a message was sent out to all Lakotas to report to their agencies or be deemed hostile, effectively risking war. They had until 31ST January 1876, three months from when the announcement was made, to comply. Travel through the winter months was not easy and getting the word to everyone was virtually impossible. So, some were unaware of the warning, others chose to ignore it.

Three armies under the command of Crook, Custer and Gibbons were sent out from different directions to round up any 'hostile' Indians. Whilst on their journey some of Crook's men came across a Cheyenne village. They drove the Indians out and burned everything to the ground. The villagers that escaped managed to find their way to Crazy Horse to seek refuge, but his camp was too small to accommodate the extra people, so he led them to Sitting Bull who was in a better position to assist them back to their feet.

We drive up a gravel track as we approach the site of the battle. To our left is a large field, this is where Crook and his men were camped at the time of the attack by the Indians. Once again, we are the only car. We pull up next to a notice board, to the side of which there is a small grassed area with some picnic tables on it. Crook's camp is now behind us, directly in front of us are some small hills, this is where the fighting took place.

The gravel track continues-on around a short loop through these hills and brings you back to the start. We follow the track so that Rose can point out some places of significance. The Indians call this battle 'The Fight Where The Girl Saved Her Brother'. A Cheyenne woman named Buffalo Calf Road Woman was fighting alongside the other warriors when she saw her brother become injured. She rode out on her horse in the heat of the battle to rescue him and bring him back to safety. As we drive slowly around the track, Rose points to the spot that this is believed to have happened. It is widely known and accepted that male Indians can be brave warriors, it is less common to consider that females could also show real courage and fearlessness in battle. Buffalo Calf Road Woman was as bold, if not more so, as any of her male counterparts. This changes my perception of Indian women, no longer do I see them solely as home makers, they too are fighters. This will become way more evident as my journey continues.

We travel full circle around the loop and arrive back at the beginning, parking next to the picnic area. We step out of the car, the only sound comes from the neighing of horses in the distance which seems kind of fitting. Rose has a large magnetic notice board that she has brought with her. She lays it flat down on one of the picnic tables and draws a map of the area that we are sat in, with the field (Crook's camp) behind us and the hills in front. She then takes out some toy cavalry men and Indians and relays the story to us by moving the pieces around the board. This is a brilliant way to get the story across. As Rose runs through the details of the battle, our eyes go from the board, to real life and then back to the board again. Rose tells the story with an excitement and passion that holds our attention throughout.

When the Indians discovered that Crook and his men were camped along the Rosebud, words were being uttered regarding a revenge attack for the Cheyenne village that had been destroyed. The chiefs opposed this, yet passions were running high amongst the young warriors and they went against the wishes of their superiors and made an attack on Crook's camp.

There is a legendary story that Rose tells us, although unsure of its authenticity, it paints a great picture in my mind. Before setting off to attack Crook's camp, warriors were calling on others to join them. They circled their camp on horses relentlessly, each time enticing more to their war party, momentum building, battle cries ringing out, women calling out the traditional high pitched "lililili", the numbers in the circle grew and grew until it was a continuous loop surrounding the camp. They then set off to Rosebud.

The Crow and Shoshoni scouts that were working on the side of Crook played a big-role in fending off the attacks from the hill to the left of where we are now sitting. This bought precious time for the soldiers to prepare themselves for battle.

The fighting lasted for over six hours. Rose informs us that it ended when Crook sent some of his men off to the east of the battle to find the camp from where the Indians had come but shortly after called them back. On returning, they arrived at the rear of the warriors. This spooked the Indians into believing that reinforcements were coming, prompting them to make their retreat, circling Crook's camp with one last show of defiance as they left.

This all happened on the 17th June 1876, a week prior to The Battle of The Little Big Horn.

On our drive back down the track to exit the site, a red-tailed hawk, the spirit bird of Crazy Horse, flies up from the long grass some forty to fifty feet in front of us. Its huge wings motion up and down as it takes off from the ground. Its prey, a light-coloured snake struggles to break free from the talons in which it is being held. A few majestic beats of its wings in unison, and it glides up onto a fence post close by. The hawk's beak comes down onto the snake, I guess to kill or at least immobilise it. Once it has its meal secured in its grasp, the bird takes off, heading across the open field towards a forest of trees in the far distance. This is as impressive as wildlife can be, yet I also find myself looking at this in a much deeper way. Before our very eyes, we have the spirit bird of Crazy Horse putting on a show at a place that he had fought in battle, in my mind I see this as a personal performance put on for us. It seems I'm becoming more spiritual with each moment that passes.

From here we make our way to Deer Medicine Rock. On our way, a pitstop would be called for as more fuel is needed, both for the car and ourselves. We have now come out of Crow country and are on the Cheyenne reservation. Rose takes us to a gas station so that we can fulfil all of our needs.

It's quite busy, yet we're noticeably the only white people here. We fill up the car and go inside to pay for our fuel and to grab something to eat. It feels as though all eyes are on us. There's a delicatessen counter at the back of the shop and we place our order. A young girl of about 18 displaying a big smile serves us and asks, "where are you guys from?" this immediately puts us at ease. When we tell her that we are English she says "wow", hands us our order and wishes us a good day.

Once back in the car Rose asks if we noticed everyone looking at us? If it was evident to you Rose, too right we noticed. The looks were more through intrigue as to who we are and why we are here than anything sinister. It does highlight however, how it feels to be massively in the minority. A little unnerving to say the least.

We pull away from the gas station, drive along the road a little way, across a set of traffic lights and then follow straight on to Deer Medicine Rock.

The Rock is on land owned by a white American man, Jim Bailey. Jim is in his 80's and his home sits at the bottom of the hill from where the rock stands. Rose goes to his house to ask permission for us to go up and take a look. He invites us into his home and asks us to sign a visitor's book. Jim chats with Rose about mutual friends within the Crow community as he shows us some things that he had found on his property. Jim is a friendly man and is clearly very proud to have Deer Medicine Rock on his land. He sees it as his duty to look after the site yet still to let people enjoy the experience of visiting. I doubt that you could find a better keeper for this sacred place.

Jim has had some problems with his hip or leg recently and is walking with a stick. Despite this, he chooses to come up in the car with us. As he gets ready to join us, Rose lights the lemon grass that she bought at the Trading Post and we smudge before we head up to the rock. The idea is to fan the smoke over your body so that as it rises it cleanses and takes away negative energy that may surround you. With Rose stressing how important this is, we are happy to carry out the ritual. As our journey has progressed, so too my interest in these beliefs. I'm not sure at this moment how convinced I am as to how much of a difference it will make but I have nothing to lose by doing it so, count me in. Freshly smudged we get into the car and make our way up the dirt track towards the top of the hill. The track has some deep divots and it becomes apparent that I have hired the right vehicle, a small SUV that is able to handle the terrain. I wouldn't have liked to have done it in anything smaller. In front of us, further up the track, a coyote appears, sees us and runs off. These are similar in colouring and shape to a wolf, although not as big. Having seen the hawk only a short while before, we are thrilled to see another beautiful wild animal.

We arrive at the top of the hill and pull up next to the rocks. From our raised position we look out across the plains where the Sundance had taken place, the only difference between the view that would have been witnessed then to what we see now is the road on which we travelled to get here, this runs directly through our eyeline.

We walk around the stone that stands up out of the ground, looking at the markings on it. We spot where Sitting Bull had etched his vision. I'm very happy to have seen this first hand, to be standing in exactly-the-same spot as the great man had once stood himself. If this is not enough, Jim points to another rock, maybe 20 feet away and shows us a marking put there by Crazy Horse!! I'm glad that Rose brought us here, albeit a little reluctantly. I feel privileged to have seen what I have.

As we look around we see a few markings that others have put on over the years, their initials and dates etc. I hope nobody else adds anymore. Everybody, not just Jim Bailey, needs to cherish what they have here. In my opinion, this is such an important place in American history and I continue to be amazed how these sites are so matter of fact. The whole experience of visiting has been somewhat surreal. We turn up, not only do we get to speak to the man that owns the land, we have his full attention, walk around a place of such significance without another sole around and then leave. I find that unbelievable.

We thank Jim for his time and for allowing us to see this historic landmark. We wish each other well before heading back to the Trading Post to drop Rose off and make our hour-long trip back to Sheridan.

Arriving back in Sheridan after a long day, we decide on pizza for tea. "There's a place just up past our hotel," I say. So, we continue on and pull into the car park of Papa Murphys. If you are American it's likely that you would have heard of these. However, if you are English, just like us, you probably have not. Nickey walks in and I follow close behind. We order and pay for our pizza and sit on a bench to wait for it. A couple of minutes pass, Nickey decides to go outside and wait. Once out there she gains my attention and beckons me to her. She then points to a sign on the door which reads 'Take and Bake'. With confused looks on our faces, we look at each other and smile. Surely not? With this, another customer leaves holding his pizza and yes, our fears are confirmed, it's raw. We have just bought an uncooked pizza with no means of cooking it! Obviously, we carry on with the charade (we would not want to look stupid), thanking them as they hand it to us, only to take it back to our hotel and give it to the receptionist to take home with her. She thought the whole thing was hilarious.

A telephone call to Papa JOHNS and our cooked pizza turns up a short-time after.

I struggle to get my head around getting a take away but then having to go home and cook it. Everyone has told us that they are lovely pizzas. We will just have to take their word for it.

Only in America.

CHAPTER ELEVEN

"TODAY IS A GOOD DAY TO DIE"

I am awoken at 4am this morning by my mobile telephone ringing. I don't get to it before it cuts off. It's midmorning back in England and a perfectly respectable time to call. I think to myself that it would have been a good idea to put my phone on silent. A text message follows soon after, I read it and respond. Although just an insignificant business call, I am now awake. I lay on my back looking up at the ceiling digesting some of the things that I've experienced over the past couple of days, putting things into some sort of order in my mind ready for our trip to the site of The Battle of The Little Big Horn, or as the Indians call it, The Battle of the Greasy Grass. Nickey lays sleeping beside me. An hour or so later, I doze back off and sleep through until the alarm goes off at 8:30.

I get out of bed and make my way into the kitchen area of our room, half eaten pizzas sit in their open boxes on the side. Nickey is already there, filling up the kettle ready for a coffee. She tidies away the remnants from last night's meal as we, with the aid of caffeine working its magic like a quick releasing potion being injected directly into our veins, fully wake up. A bowl of cereal followed by a refreshing shower and I'm ready to face the world once more.

We set off on our commute to the Trading Post, quickly becoming creatures of habit, on arrival we have a drink and wait for Rose to arrive just as we had the day before.

Rose has already taken a group tour early this morning, she gets to us at about 10:45 and we make the short trip to the site of The Battle of The Little Big Horn. As we pull up to the booth where they would usually take your entrance fee, Rose shows her ticket from earlier and we gain free entry yet again. We drive into the car park, on our right there are rows and rows of beautifully kept headstones in a faultless, uniform formation set in perfectly mowed grass that could not have been any greener if each blade had been individually painted to the desired colour. The American flag flies high and proud. This cemetery is for people that have lost their lives serving in the military.

Rose leads us to the visitor's centre and tells of an information video that plays at regular intervals throughout the day. We walk in, Rose chats with friends that work here. She used to work here herself before going it alone. The film has already started so we decide to come back for one of the later showings, we can then view it from the beginning. Nickey and I walk around looking at pictures, memorabilia and information boards that are placed around the centre. One of the facts that attracts my attention is regarding the amount of people that had died in this battle that were not born in America. Out of the 840 people that died on the side of the U.S, 368 were foreign born. One hundred and twenty-five were born in Germany, 128 in Ireland and another 53 in the United Kingdom. So, other than 15 from Canada, the rest of the 368 were born in Europe. Rose explains that a lot of the people that fought had found themselves in a position where joining the military had become their best option. Having made their way to America to find their riches and search for gold, it didn't take long to realise that things were not quite so straight forward. Arriving in the U.S with very little, joining the military became a way of getting fed, clothed and earning a bit of money. So, although I don't hold much sympathy for the likes of Custer, I do have a little for the soldiers that, through circumstances that worked against them, found themselves in these battles.

For the time being we leave the visitors centre and walk the short distance up to the monument put in place to commemorate where

Custer and a group of his men had fallen, the actual spot of the 'Last Stand'. Small headstones mark the positions where individuals lost their lives. These are scattered across the hills that surround the centre. White stones represent the American soldiers, red ones for the Native American warriors. Originally more were spread around this large area, yet some have now been brought closer to the visitor centre. As we look at some of these and read the names upon them, Nickey points out the different terminology on two of the stones that we see as we walk. The white one states that the soldier had been 'killed', yet the red one said the warrior had 'died'. I'm not sure how much you can read into this, but it feels as though there is a subtle seed planted into our brains. 'Killed' reads very differently to 'died'.

A purpose-built road leads up from the monument to Reno's Hill, where some of the fighting took place. We will take a drive up there shortly but first we wander across the road to look at another monument, this one put up on behalf of the Indians. Shockingly this was not until 2003!! Better late than never I guess.

It is too far to walk to Reno's Hill from where we are, so we go back down to the car and drive the winding road up. Horses run free by the side of the road and across the open land that surrounds us. There are a couple of laybys that you can pull into on the way up, but we don't stop, driving slowly so to remain respectful to the people that lost their lives here, we continue to the top. We park up and walk along the path towards one of the viewpoints that overlook the valley below. A number of different paths head to different points, all in close proximity, with similar views. There is grass between each pathway and as we walk along, we see the small head and part of the body of a snake, the rest of it is hidden in the grass. Unsure of what type of snake this is, we take no chances, back up, choose a different path and walk the short distance to the end.

From this position we get a good view of what would have been seen by Custer and his men as they approached the camp. The valley below is large, however, a substantial amount of it is obscured by trees. Only being able to see a small section of the camp, apparently led to Custer underestimating how many Indians were here. Depending on whom you speak to, the number of warriors differs greatly. It seems convenient for the losers of this particular-battle to say that there were up to ten thousand, this somehow leaves them with a little credibility. After all, if this was the case, they were well out numbered. Others claim, based on the amount of tipis and the average number of warriors per tipi, the figure was more like eighteen hundred. The truth is probably somewhere between these figures, although I'm tempted to think that it is closer to the lesser number.

Custer cut an imposing figure, with long red hair and a matching, finely groomed beard. He had an ego to match his appearance and liked to do things his way. Following the Battle Of The Rosebud, Crook was temporarily out of action. Custer and Gibbon had met up to discuss their next plan of action. They set off in different directions with their respective armies to round up the Indians, the last words Gibbon uttered to his supposed ally were, "Now don't be greedy Custer. Wait for us to arrive." To which he replied with a smile, "I will not."

On approaching the camp, Custer and his men could see dust coming up from the area inhabited by the Indians and believed that they were making a hasty retreat. This had often been the way in the past, yet on this occasion it was just the women, children and elders that were looking to escape. Unaware of this, Custer made the call to attack and not to wait for reinforcements. This was a mistake on two parts, firstly as mentioned, there were greater numbers of Lakota and Cheyenne warriors than he had anticipated and secondly, he never gave his men time to recover from the tiring journey that they had endured to get here. Custer led his weary soldiers straight into a battle and on this occasion the Indians did not scatter. With the words, "Today is a good day to die," going around the camp along with the extra confidence and belief that had been gained from Sitting Bull's vision, the warriors were ready. This time they came out to fight.

Custer ordered Reno, his second in command, to attack from the south, while he would take his men to hit the camp from the far side to the north. During the time it took Custer to get into position, Reno came under fierce resistance from the Indians. The reports that came out of the Indian camp were that there was complete chaos amongst the men on both sides. Horses were scared by the gun fire and were jumping and rearing up. The shots that were being fired were mostly going into the air but there is also a big chance that a number of men were killed by their own people. Amongst the disarray the Indians got the upper hand. There are strong rumours that Bloody Knife, one of Reno's Arikara scouts, had been shot whilst standing beside him, this led to Reno having a brief loss of composure. During the moments of chaos that followed, he ordered his men to mount, dismount and remount their horses in the space of a few seconds. Reno and his men were forced to make a retreat and take stock on the hill which we are currently standing on.

After a short while, fighting started at the other end of camp from where Custer was now attacking. The Indians turned their attention to this area leaving Reno with some time to decide on his next move. It is believed that Reno claimed to be unaware that Custer was engaged in combat and therefore made no attempt to support him.

We all know that Custer met his fate that day. This is the part where, in the movies, Custer stands strong, cutting a defiant figure, still fighting right until the very end. The fact of the matter is, nobody really knows exactly how it happened or even, who killed him. Many like to credit this to Crazy Horse but this could just be the romantic finale that the Indians wish for. There is also a book in the North Dakota State Library in which Chief White Bull talks of being the one that killed Custer, although, this too cannot be verified. I wonder, in the heat of the battle with the craziness going on all around, does the killer himself even know?

From here, with Custer no longer an issue, the Indians made their way back to Reno's hill and kept the attack going until nightfall. They continued at sun rise the next day and through into the afternoon. Eventually the Indians left Reno and the remainder of his men and moved out of the camp. The next morning, Reno and his battle worn troops made their way closer to the river and were found by Gibbon and his men.

It seems strange that, considering Reno had not offered support to Custer amid his claims of being unaware of the battle taking place, an inquiry saw thirteen of Reno's men awarded for bravery. Conveniently, there was never any mention of Reno's lapse in composure.

Heading back up the pathway from where we came, Rose and I hear a very loud swishing sound that resembles somebody shaking maracas close by. We both jump back and are immediately aware that this is the sound of a rattle snake. Nickey does not hear it and momentarily continues, oblivious to any danger. Rose and I call her back, I reach out and grab her arm realising that she is heading straight for the diamond back literally a few feet in front of us. By the noise that it makes, I'm guessing that it may not be too pleased with us for interrupting it sunning itself on the path, tucked up close enough to the grass so that it couldn't instantly be seen. Still unaware of what the problem is, Nickey becomes hysterical, "What is it? What is it?" she cries with tears welling up in her eyes. From a safe distance, we point out the snake. Now far enough away for it not to cause us any harm, Nickey reveals that her first fear was that it was a bee!! A bee?! We all laugh at her over reaction and even more so when we see how quickly she calms down after being made aware that it was in fact a deadly snake. It appears Nickey would rather take on a rattle snake over a bee any day. Good luck with that love.

The problem for us now is that there is no way past and we have no choice but to sit it out. Watching our slivery friend's every move, we wait. He is in control here. We could be waiting for five minutes or five hours. While we wait, I snap a couple of photographs to show my friends how close we came to this deadly creature. Fortunately, he's not too keen on us being in his vicinity and does not take long before he heads off into the grass. Phew, we live to fight another day.

The adrenalin in our bodies is at an elevated level, as we head back to the car we see a bench and take the opportunity to sit for a few moments to regain our composure. It's not every day that you have a close encounter with a rattlesnake, not in my world anyway.

As we sit on the bench, we talk excitedly about what has just happened. Rose tells us that in her seven years of coming up here for tours, it is also her first time of experiencing such an episode. Our analysis is that, with it being the end of the season, it is quiet yet the weather is still warm. The snake, that would have stayed away during the summer months due to large numbers of visitors, was enjoying the peaceful moments to warm itself on the sun-baked footpath. That said, I'm not totally convinced that seeing them up here is quite as rare as we are led to believe. My feeling is, it might not be good for business for potential customers to believe that this may happen on their visits. For me however, it added to our experience and I would not change it in any way. Would it prevent me from coming again? Definitely-not, although admittedly I may be more vigilant of what is around me.

We drive back down to the visitor's centre and catch one of the afternoon showings of the information film that we had missed earlier. It lasts approximately half an hour and reiterates the things that Rose has told us about the battle. The 4am phone call starts to catch up with me and as I watch the screen my eyes begin to close, an afternoon power nap would be nice. I manage to stay awake and watch to the end.

Our time with Rose is coming to an end. We have enjoyed the days that we have spent with her. It has certainly been an adventure and the memories made are very fond ones. Before we say our last good bye, Rose needs to show me where I have to go tomorrow morning to meet my guide for my much-anticipated horseback ride. Although I have not ridden for a few years, I'm nervously excited at the prospect of getting off the beaten track and seeing the whole thing from the saddle of a horse, just as they had around the time of the battle. Sadly, Nickey has an allergy to horses and is not able to share in this adventure. She makes all the usual noises of disappointment but secretly I think she is relieved that she will not be taking part in this section of the journey.

We take a couple of photographs of ourselves posing with Rose in front of the colourful tipis outside of the Trading Post before we leave her for the last time.

As I drive away, I look across the dashboard and the lemon grass that we had used to smudge ourselves the day before sits tucked up against the windscreen on the passenger side. I glance at Nickey and say, "You know what we didn't do this morning?"

"What?" Nickey asks.

"We never smudged. After everything that Rose told us before we went to Deer Medicine Rock, we should have smudged. The snake encounter may have never happened if we had."

We may have left Rose in the carpark at the Trading Post, but part of her spiritual side has rubbed off onto us and we will carry that around forever. In fact, more than I would have ever thought possible.

CHAPTER TWELVE

PALE RIDER

So, Rose has awoken a spiritual side in me that I never realised existed. I have not found God, if you speak to me I'm the same person that I have always been. But something inside of me is now different. I have a total belief in the 'mitakuye oyasin' thing, I believe that we are all related, we are all connected within the Universe. Since my visit, things have happened that are difficult to explain. Although the details of these shall remain personal to me, it's important that I mention them as they have become a part of my journey. To some, this sort of thing is all mumbo jumbo, to others (myself included) there is something to it.

After our encounter with the rattle snake yesterday, I've become a little more nervous of my horseback ride. When I stir during the night I look at my watch to check on the time. It says that it's ten to nine, which it clearly is not. At a guess it's more like 1am. It appears that my watch has stopped. My ride out is scheduled for 9am the next morning, which leads to my mind racing away. Is my watch stopping just before this specific time a warning, maybe some sort of message? My mind goes back to my conversation with Rose prior to our visit to Deer Medicine Rock, "Is it because you are a Crow?" replays in my head.

"And because you are white", I can hear Rose's voice clearly as I lay thinking.

I start to wonder how a horse will react if a rattle snake is beneath its feet. Will it rare up? Could it throw me to the ground? If I'm thrown off, I would be on the floor with the snake. This could be bad. Should I even go on this horse ride?

I try to reassure myself that all will be fine. The western saddles are much safer than the ones back in England. It's far harder to fall from one of these. The horses spend their whole lives in the area that I will be riding, everything will be okay. I will make sure of it by smudging before we leave the hotel carpark. Something that a couple of weeks ago I would have seen as crazy is now going to save me from certain death at the hands of a deadly snake. Funny how my attitude has changed.

We load the car as it is time for another new destination. After the horse ride we will be heading up to Yellowstone for a couple of nights.

Once the car is loaded, we take the lemon grass from the dashboard and set light to it. As soon as it starts to simmer we waft the smoke over ourselves. I now have nothing to fear. I can enjoy my day free from worry.

We make the trip from Sheridan to the Trading Post for one last time. We go into the shop as I have no gloves and at this time of year, in these parts, the mornings are a bit chilly. I decide to tough it out as the gloves in the Trading Post are a little expensive, after all, I only really need them for a couple of hours and do not want to pay too much.

The place for the horse ride is only a mile or so up the road. I'm to meet with a guy called Curtis RealBird at his home, which is a small ranch. As we pull up in the drive, Curtis comes out to meet us. He is a Crow in his early 60's. It's easy to read the type of person Curtis is and I do so quickly. He comes across as a strong character, but he also has a dry sense of humour. I instantly like him.

Curtis greets us as we get out of the car and says that he had not prepared the horses just yet as it was common for people not to show up. I don't let on that I had been spooked the day before and nearly never made it myself. Instead I say, "Really?" looking shocked that people would not take this opportunity, "I have been looking forward to this for ages." This is actually true, it's only because of yesterday's events that I have become a little paranoid. He starts to walk towards the stables where a couple of horses are tied up outside. "Where are you guys staying at?" he asks. "Sheridan, but from here we move on to Yellowstone," I answer. Curtis looks straight at me, "Why are you staying in Sheridan? You should have stayed in Hardin," a place that is close by, "We are not savages you know," he smiles. He knows exactly what he has done here. He's obviously pulling my leg and making me squirm a little. "We just went where we were put," in typical English fashion I pass the buck straight onto someone else, in this case our tour guide Sarah. We both smile in acknowledgement of how we played out this little encounter.

Nickey asks how long he thinks we will be as she will go for a coffee and wait at the Trading Post, then come back to get me. "About two hours, I don't want to kill him," Curtis laughs as he speaks. We laugh too, mine tinged with a slight nervousness. I nod in agreement as this will be my first time on a horse in a while, years in fact. The western saddles are a lot more comfortable, but it is all relative. A couple of hours sounds fine to me.

Curtis and I lead two chestnut brown horses by the reins over to where they will be tacked up. Once they are ready to go, Curtis goes inside to put his boots on and asks me if I need gloves. "Oh yes please, if you have some," I say, glad that I never spent a load of money on buying a pair. As he walks inside, I have the reins of 'Trow', my horse for the trip. At this point I felt that I was in control of my four-legged friend for as I led him over to this spot, he willingly done what I wanted. While Curtis is inside I try to pull Trow over to one side, he does not budge. I pull the reins again, he is having none of it, feet firmly on the ground, he pulls back against me with his head. Perhaps I won't be the boss then! Animals are not as dumb as we humans believe. Trow clearly knows that Curtis is his master and when he's around he behaves as he is expected, however, when Curtis goes inside, he is not so willing to comply to my wishes.

Curtis returns and hands me a pair of leather cowboy gloves. Other than missing a hat, I now look the part. We jump on our horses, say goodbye to Nickey then walk along the track that takes us out of Curtis's yard and through a gate which leads us to the Little Big Horn. Within minutes of setting off we are riding our horses across the river. I'm not sure why crossing the water feels so special, but it does. I don't know if I'm now in control of Trow or whether he is just going through the motions but as we enter the water I steer him to where I want him to go and he obliges. The river is quite deep and almost reaches my feet as we make the crossing. When we get to the other side, I kick a little harder to get Trow up the short but steep bank. Throughout this ride I constantly kick Trow to keep him moving yet Curtis keeps telling me to be firmer with him, not sure what more I can do really. Curtis drops behind me for a moment and taps Trow's backside, this makes him give a little spurt of energy. Trow is by no means an old cart horse and is perfect for the level of rider that I am. He may like to dictate the pace, but I can live with that.

When getting to know someone for the first time you look for a common ground on which you can strike up a conversation, for men at least, this is quite often sport. Curtis asks if I'm a rugby or soccer fan. I tell him that my passion is "soccer". I do watch some of the big international rugby matches but that's about it. We are both in agreement that it is a tough man's game. He has watched a little Spanish soccer and mentions Ronaldo and Messi and how good they are. I tell him that I'm a Tottenham fan, I don't think he has heard of them. We speak about the crazy money sports stars earn both sides of the Atlantic and how easy it is for them to lose touch with reality.

Curtis leads and I follow close behind as we climb a steep rocky slope. We walk along the ridge at the top that runs parallel with the road we had driven on the previous day from the visitors centre to Reno's Hill. Other than a motor home followed closely by another vehicle, the only other person that we see during our ride is a cyclist. He has stopped at one of the laybys to read the information board. Curtis calls down from the ridge, "Hey, how's it going?" The man, dressed in cycling attire looks up, "Yeah good. Shame these people have to drive their motor homes along here!" Apparently, the other vehicle that was following was in the same party. "They could have left it at the bottom and all gone up in the car.," as he speaks he holds out his hands in a questioning manner, these inconsiderate people had ruined his experience a little, something that could have easily been avoided. I can't say that it bothered me in the same way, it hadn't even registered in my mind until he mentioned it. I'm sure the 'guilty' party probably never gave it another thought either. Curtis asks where he is from. "Chicago", he shouts back. "Ticking this off my bucket list," he adds.

Now I don't have a bucket list, well not in the physical sense, as in I have never written anything down but if I did have one, then my trip would be on it too.

Curtis points out that he has done the hard part as he is now on his way back down the hill. The road up is one that you only really appreciate the incline of when you have to climb it under your own steam, such as running, cycling or even walking. We had the luxury of the car yesterday, today Trow is taking the strain.

"Well enjoy the rest of your trip. Have a good day," Curtis calls down. "You too," the cyclist raises his hand to wave farewell as we continue-on with our respective journeys.

When I think about this brief encounter, I wonder how it looked through the eyes of the cyclist. As he lives out one of the dreams on his bucket list, cycling along this particular pass at the site of the Battle of The Little Big Horn, upon a ridge on the other side of the road, two guys appear on horse-back, one a Native American dressed as a modern-day cowboy and me. As I stated before, other than the hat being missing, I look the part. He does not know that I'm an Englishman on a riding trip. In my (biased, even delusional) opinion, I could pass as a ranch hand. I hope that it added to his experience and helped him forget about his displeasure at the motor home blotting the landscape.

As we move away from the road, I can see for miles. We are surrounded by open fields in small hill formations. In the distance, half way up one of these hills there's a group of horses. Curtis calls out in a loud voice, within a second or two the horses start to run. Wild horses running free is a beautiful sight, their manes flowing in the wind, it is a sight that epitomises the spirit of freedom. I am amazed that they could hear him from such a distance, I begin to mention this to Curtis, but he stops me midsentence and points to some more horses that are no more than small dots about as far away as my eyes could see. As he points, these take flight too. Unbelievable. Curtis uses this to point out, "And Reno says that he couldn't hear the battle going on with Custer."

Job done Curtis, you have proved your point without any doubt whatsoever.

During our short-time together, Curtis and I talk about many things. He asks where we have visited on this trip, adding, "I guess you have seen that face in the rock?" My understanding at the time was that he was talking about Mount Rushmore, "Yeah, we thought we would take a look as we were there," I reply. "Stupid ain it? Ruined a perfectly good rock," he answers his own question in the same sentence. I now think that as he said 'face' and not 'faces' he probably actually meant the Crazy Horse monument. As I said in a previous chapter, there are mixed views on this. That said, let us not forget that Curtis is a Crow and Crazy Horse was an Oglala Lakota.

He also asks what sort of house I live in. I explain that we don't have the same space that they have and that I live in a three-bedroom semi of no real-size. I believe that Curtis would feel like a battery hen if he had to live in my house.

With his land and lifestyle, along with Native American tradition, he enjoys hunting for his food. "Do you ever hunt?" he asks. "No, I would struggle with killing anything," I see his face and pre-empt his next comment, before he says it I continue, "I know what you are going to say, yes I do eat meat, but I just couldn't see myself killing the animal. I'm happy to let someone else do that for me," I smile. "I guess if I had to do it I would, but given the choice, it's not for me." Curtis smiles back with a look that says he thinks I am a typical town/city type. I cannot argue with that, it's a fair judgement.

We chat further as we make our way back towards Curtis's home. "Have you tried the Indian tacos yet? They do real good ones up at the Trading Post," Curtis says with some enthusiasm. "No, we haven't. What are they?"

"They are nothing like Mexican tacos, they are a fry bread," he tells me. I now know that they are frequently referred to as 'fry bread' also. Curtis continues, "You should try some before you head off to Yellowstone." I nod, yet think it's still a bit early for a big lunch but make a note to have one at some stage whilst we are here.

"Where in Yellowstone are you staying?"

"Cody."

He tells me his favourite restaurant in this town and recommends that we go there for a steak. I make a note of that too. I love a nice steak.

We arrive back at the river and before we cross, Curtis asks if I would like him to take a couple of photographs. I hand him my phone and tell him to take care as my whole life is in this little device. He laughs as he takes it carefully from my grip. As Trow and I make our way from one side to the other, Curtis snaps some pictures.

As we go back through the gate and head up the track, Nickey is waiting. Curtis and I, sat on our horses, walk side by side as we approach. Nickey clicks away on the camera. These are some of my favourite photos.

We dismount our trusted steeds and Curtis ties them up. He has another trip out with a television company in a couple of hours so leaves them tacked up.

There's a small grandstand a hundred meters or so from Curtis's property set back a little way from the river. This is for spectators to watch the re-enactment of the battle that the RealBirds stage on the anniversary weekend every year. We have enjoyed our time together and Curtis tells me that I need to return to watch this for myself. Maybe I will do just that.

Before we leave, I hand Curtis a tip, as I had done with our other guides, "That'll work," is the straight, no nonsense response that I expect and get from him. "Would you like to keep the gloves?" He asks. "Can I?"

"Sure."

I've had a great-time and for a couple of hours I have fulfilled every schoolboy of my era's dream of riding out across the plains at the site of the Battle of The Little Big Horn, just me and my Indian buddy. I leave with my cowboy gloves, a whole load of great memories and of course, a bit of a sore backside.

CHAPTER THIRTEEN

YELLOWSTONE

It's now late Saturday morning and we have a five-hour drive to get to Cody. This journey is pretty non-eventful, more a case of just getting from one place to another. Driving around the outskirts of some of the bigger towns and cities such as Billings in Montana, it reminds me of similar places back home, with dual carriageways that bypass the town centre. However, as you would expect, with the buildings becoming fewer, the mountains and open land more regular, the closer we get to Yellowstone, the nicer the scenery becomes.

Our drive takes us back into Wyoming and we arrive in Cody at around 5pm. It is another typical north, mid-western American town but with more of a tourist feel. It is named after Buffalo Bill Cody as he was one of its original creators. Buffalo Bill was known for his wild west show that he travelled the world performing, even visiting Southampton where I currently live. I was unaware of this until, whilst having a conversation with one of my clients, he told me how his great grandfather had befriended him when they were here and was given gifts such as whips and an Indian penny that are still in his family today.

The show consisted of staged cowboy and Indian encounters and famously had recruits such as Sitting Bull and Annie Oakley (Annie get your gun) in its entourage. I do not believe that this was a happy time for Sitting Bull. Being paraded like some sort of pantomime villain for such a proud man must have been soul destroying. His life certainly was no pantomime, neither was he a villain. It was during his travels with this show that he saw many poor white people, some just young children, begging in the streets, his comment in true Sitting Bull style, "…and you say that WE are uncivilised!"

Our hotel is at the far end of the town, we make our way there and check in. All of the hotels that we have stayed in have been nice but this one had more of a homely feel. We were happy with our room and excited to be spending some time in Yellowstone. If I'm honest, my excitement is largely based on the chance of seeing a bear. There are warning signs all over the place telling us not to feed them, so surely there must be plenty around. Tomorrow we are driving through the park on our way up to visit Old Faithful, the world-famous geyser, it will take four hours each way, more than ample time to see a grizzly.

Tonight, we take Curtis's advice and visit the restaurant that he recommended. It's only a small place and is busy when we arrive. There are no tables available, but they take our name and tell us to return in an hour. That is fine with us, it gives us a chance to take a walk along the main street and look in the shops as we go. Some have closed early as it's getting close to the end of the holiday season and there are not too many people around. The ones that are seem to all be in the restaurant.

As we wander from shop to shop, I see a nice hand painted, Native American drum that I like but the price is very high, and way more than I'm prepared to pay. However, Nickey buys something in the same shop and we get chatting to the owners. They tell us that they are just about to close-down for the winter and are selling things at discounted prices. We make a very low offer for the drum and although they do not accept it, we manage to beat them down (excuse the pun) from the original price and I walk away with it under my arm and a smile on my face.

Back at the restaurant, we take our seats and order our steaks. As we wait for our meals we take out our phones to have a little look at Facebook to see what is happening at home. We point out various posts from friends and family to one another. I see that the only 'Facebook friend' that I have from my secondary school days has commented on another ex-school colleague's status regarding her going on a trip to Disney. As I read through the posts I see a couple of other guys having a go at each other. One had been bullied by the other during our school years. I can empathise as I too suffered at the hands of the same person, although originally, we had been very good friends. Over thirty years have passed, and I've put those days behind me, clearly this other victim has not been able to do so. The fact that he has carried it around with him for so many years shows how horrible and deeply affected people can become. Although personally, I do feel that it has made me stronger in my adult life. Nobody bullies me anymore.

Nickey and I discuss this a little, reliving how awful it is to be a victim. With our current mindset being focused strongly on the plight of the American Indians, we see some similarities, although on a completely different scale. The American Governments treatment of the Native Americans takes bullying to another level, there can be no bigger example in the history of time.

I regularly get asked, with regards to me writing this book, 'why do you care so much?' I believe a part of it is because of these unpleasant experiences from my school days. Perhaps I have not moved on in the way that I thought. I tend to struggle watching others being treated badly, always feeling the need to step in. These things from my past have formed the personality I have today.

Our steaks arrive, they look and taste good. Cooked exactly as we have asked. Thank you for the recommendation Curtis. Darkness has fallen on Cody during our time in the restaurant, the warmth from the sun no longer evident, we put our hoodies on as we head back to our hotel.

The following morning, we prepare for a long journey in the car with a hearty breakfast. Driving four hours each way in one day seems like an awful lot, however, when I think about it, what better way to see Yellowstone than to drive through it. My perception of the day ahead changes from looking at Old Faithful as a destination to more incorporating our time on the road as part of the whole experience.

In 1872, President Ulysses S. Grant signed a bill to make Yellowstone the world's first federally protected national park. In relation to Native Americans, the park has some myths and stories surrounding it. Yellowstone is in Shoshone territory, although other tribes have ancestral links here. Many tribes would come here to hunt. The most commonly known myth is that the Native Americans were afraid of the park because of the geysers. With hot steaming water bursting out of the ground up to 200 feet in the air at sporadic intervals, you could see that this could quite easily be the case. However, it is believed that this is not true, in reality the whites had tried to rid the park of Indians and the story was concocted so that other white settlers would believe that it was a safe place to visit, without worrying about encounters with Natives.

As we drive out of Cody for our day of exploring, our concentration levels are up and we look hard to see if we can see any bears. Every time the road crosses small rivers and streams, we look to see if there are any on the river bends. Shallow water glistens in the sun as it runs down over rocks and stones, it all looks beautiful, but there are no bears. We look in through the trees as we drive through woodland, there are no bears. I'm beginning to wonder if there are as many as they claim or whether the belief that they may be seen attracts visitors to the park.

We come to a toll booth, an entrance fee is to be paid if we are to enter what I assume to be the heart of the park. A friendly man takes my money and asks if we are having a good day? "Yes, great thanks. Although, we haven't seen any bears yet," I reply.

I tell him that we are heading up to Old Faithful and he says that we might be lucky and see one on our way.

Our drive has us climb up through winding roads with many bends. The drop from the side is quite severe, making me cautious not to go too fast. Through the clearings you can see more trees in the distance, the tops of which are obscured by clouds.

We have only seen the occasional car on our drive so far, then out of the blue and for no apparent reason, close to a bend that we are approaching, there are a number of vehicles parked by the side of the road. "I wonder what's going on here?" I say to Nickey. As we get closer I can see that there are people down at the edge of the trees with cameras set up, all facing into the woods. "I reckon there's a bear," I say in an excited voice. I park up by the other cars, take the camera and we make our way down to where the other people are gathered. We weave our way through to get a clear view, the only speaking is done in whispers. And there, through a clearing in the trees, a beautiful grizzly and her amazing cub!! The mother, impressive in size and stature, her baby, so cute, both covered in thick fur. Even though we know how dangerous these animals can be, I still feel a slight urge to go over and give them both a big hug. We stand quietly watching for a bit as they sit, Mum with her back to us. Then they begin to move, and the cameras start clicking in the same way that the papperazzi snap an 'a' list celebrity. They only move a few steps then settle again. This pattern repeats itself a few times before we drag ourselves away to continue with our day. Whatever else happens over the coming hours, I will be happy, I have seen a grizzly and her cub in Yellowstone.

As we carry on to Old Faithful we pass a lake on our left, on the edges of which, steam and gasses rise up out of the ground. They are evident not just by sight but also by smell. They release a gaseous odour that has us covering our noses for a few moments. The usual, predictable joke, "is that you?" pursues. We both laugh as our hands cover the bottom half of our faces.

Old Faithful is aptly named. It erupts without fail every ninety or so minutes. Many people come to see it, today there are two or three coach loads of Japanese tourists here to witness it. As we make our way closer to where the geysers are, we walk past a large bison that is stood at the side of the footpath grazing. Once again, we keep a safe distance. I've seen clips of these animals chasing visitors around this very site. We leave him be in the hope that he will do the same with us (leave us be that is, not chase us around Yellowstone).

A notice board inside the visitor's centre predicts the time of the next eruption. It tells us to expect it to be at around 1:30pm but it could be ten minutes either side. We check our watches and see that it's just after 1, we are lucky, not long until showtime. We have a brief wander around before heading outside to take up a good-position from which to observe this world famous natural extravaganza. Within moments, Old Faithful performs her fascinating show for us. Starting gently and building up to a powerful crescendo, it shoots scalding water (up to 250 degrees Fahrenheit) high up into the air continuously for a few minutes, as it does so, the audience look on in awe. Accompanied by whoops and cheers from the people around us, we watch natures very own version of a Roman Candle firework, except with water in place of flames and way more spectacular. It is quite something. It dies down gradually and peters out to a stop. It may only be a short show, yet it is a magical one. Although it will be on again in another 90 minutes, we will not be here to see it as we leave to make our way back to Cody for our last evening there.

Our time in Yellowstone may have been brief yet we were happy that we saw plenty in a short amount of time. This park, all 2.2 million acres of it, throws up so many natural wonders. It is beautiful and mystical, just amazing. It becomes another place that I would love to return to at a later date. For now, however, our schedule has us on the move once more. Our next destination will be our last before we head back to Denver in preparation for our flight home.

CHAPTER FOURTEEN

WIND RIVER

We arrived in Denver two weeks ago, yet there is something that is associated strongly with modern day Native America that we are still to experience, and that is to visit a casino. This is about to change, as our next stop has us staying at Wind River Casino on the Wind River Reservation.

The reservation is shared by two tribes, the Eastern Shoshone and the Northern Arapaho. The hotel, owned by the Northern Arapaho, is modern and has all you could want or need, if one of those happens to be to play slot machines, chance your arm at a game of Black Jack or maybe Roulette, then you will not be disappointed.

The gambling laws in America are totally different on the reservations to that of the rest of the country. The reservations have their own sovereignty and therefore it is not easy to implement the same laws. The casinos are also a great example that Native Americans are more than capable of running successful businesses.

Shortly after checking in to our room, we head downstairs to explore. I'm not big on gambling and have never visited Las Vegas. This is probably as close as I've come both in geographical terms as well as in the experiencing that whole bright lights, ringing bells, sirens going etc that come from thousands of slot machines being in one room. Cold drinks and tea/coffee are all complimentary as are certain snacks. As it is open 24/7, there is absolutely no reason for you to leave, until you run out of money of course!

There are also a couple of restaurants just set off from the casino at the rear. We walk around to where they are situated to assess our options for our evening meal. There's a board outside one of them advertising 'Rack of Lamb' as tonight's special. Mmmm…rack of lamb…our minds drift off in the way of the Bisto kids in the television adverts from the past…mint sauce, gravy, roast potatoes…sold. That's what we are having for dinner. A nice change from the steaks, burgers or pizzas that have made up a substantial part of our diet since our arrival. I'm going to have my work cut out in the gym when I get home to get rid of these extra pounds.

When ordering our rack of lamb, we are asked if we want fries or mash with it. So much for the roast potatoes. It arrives, there is no gravy, instead it is covered in a thick barbeque sauce. Oh well, it was a nice thought.

After our dinner we take the plunge and throw ourselves at the mercy of the slot machines. To encourage people to play, the casino offers new members a free $5 credit to use. We take advantage of this, so have ten dollars to play with between us. We find a machine that we like (more to the point, understand), we grab a (free)coffee and take our seats. There is an option on the machines as to how much you would like to pay per spin, ranging from 25 cents to $3 (this varies with each machine), the amount that you can win increases with the size of your stake. You guessed it, we played for 25 cents. A lady comes to play the machine next to us which is the same as the one that we are on. Within a few minutes she wins just under $500, bells ring and lights flash. She looks at us and apologises. "That's fine, well done. We are only playing for pennies anyway," I say, partly pleased for her although a little bit envious. "Oh, so am I," she tells me as she clicks another $1 spin. It seems that we have different opinions on the meaning of 'pennies'.

Nickey and I set ourselves a spending limit of $20 that we would add to our free credits, with the understanding that once gone we would stop. On the other hand, should the money accumulate to the amount of $50, we would also walk away.

82

Forty-five minutes later we leave the casino $20 down. Totally as expected. Time for bed.

Our final trip out is to be with Sarah and involves a few hours exploring the Wind River Reservation. Sarah, in appearance is a white American lady in her late thirties. She is married to a Native American man and also claims to have a Native American history. She is the owner of the company with whom we booked our tour.

Sarah suggests that she drives our car, she is insured, and it is easier than her having to give me directions. I agree and hand her the key. We head out to see the Wind River Reservation.

Our first stop is a short visit to a centre that shows and sells Native American arts and crafts. I buy a decorative shaft that has a bird's claw at the bottom and fur around the shaft itself. These are used during dances and ceremonies. From here we drive a little way up the road and stop again, this time at a grave yard, a place that resembles the types of cemeteries that you would see in western movies. Small in size, dusty and a little unkempt. This is the resting place of the Shoshone Chief Washakie.

Chief Washakie is known for his signing of the 1851 treaty at Fort Laramie.

There is also a legendary story of this chief that we are about to learn. As we continue our exploration of the reservation, Sarah pulls up by the side of the road to show us Crow Heart Butte that stands in the distance. Chief Washakie's name comes up once more. Sarah tells us of a battle that took place here between the Shoshones along with their allies the Bannocks against the Crows in 1866. This was regarding a dispute over hunting land that had been given to the different tribes at separate treaties. The battle lasted for four days but with no clear winner seeming to be apparent, the tribes decided that the best way to settle it would be to have a one on one fight to the death between Washakie and the Crow Chief, Big Robber. This was hard fought but Washakie eventually came away victorious. It is said that after his victory, Chief Washakie cut out the heart of his rival and placed it on his lance. This is where the name 'Crow Heart Butte' came from.

It's also believed that Chief Washakie later ate the heart of Chief Big Robber. This may sound gruesome, but it was in fact a mark of respect. Washakie had seen his opponent as a brave warrior and believed that by eating his heart he would be placing that courage into his own body.

Today's trip out is only a short one, this is perfect as Nickey is not feeling very well and not up for doing much. A case of exploring the reservation a little, which we manage to do. We see more clusters of homes and more obvious poverty (although not to the extent of Pine Ridge). We also get to sample our first Indian Taco.

As Curtis had said on our ride out, it is not like a Mexican Taco. In appearance, it looks more like a thick naan bread with mince, grated cheese and sauces on the top. It is golden in colour and fills the plate. Sarah tells us to save some as once you have finished eating it as a main course, they bring you honey which you can dip it in and it serves as a dessert too. Saving some would not be a problem, there is no way that I would be able to eat the whole thing.

It was nice as a main but even nicer with the honey, tasting a lot like a doughnut.

After eating, we head back to our hotel.

We have reached the end of our day and effectively the end of our tour. Tomorrow morning, we will be making our way back to Denver for two nights before heading back home to England.

The next day, our drive back has us reflecting on the past couple of weeks. "What did you like the most?" Nickey asks me. "That's impossible to answer. It has all been amazing," I reply, Nickey nods in agreement. "How about you?" I ask, "Same," she answers. We look out at the beautiful surroundings on this final drive. As was the case at the start of the book, there are no other vehicles, we are alone. Some white-tailed deer run across the road in front of us and I slow down to ensure that I do not hit them. Nickey and I look at each other and smile. We are both richer from our experiences, not in the financial meaning of the word, but in so many other ways.

Back in Denver we have a full day to fill, I look on-line to search for things to do here. Even the locals struggle to come up with anything that does not involve heading out of town for winter sports such as skiing etc. We end up spending the day looking around the shops. It's wet and miserable, great preparation for us going back to England.

The evening of our flight arrives. We sit in Denver airport waiting to board our plane and head home. What an amazing experience. We are very blessed to have these memories to take with us. One last check-in on Facebook to tell everyone that we are on our way back. A final message from Reuben reads…

"Toksa ache wanchinyankin kte lo", which translated means, "when we see each other again we will speak".

I'm looking forward to it already.

CHAPTER FIFTEEN

BACK HOME

Well I am now back in England and have been writing for a few months. With that comes a continuation of learning and effectively, my journey. The things that I've seen are still clear in my mind. On returning home from the trip, people ask me how it was? Did we have a good time? To which I answer that it was amazing and thank them for asking. Then I find questions being asked such as, "do they still live on reservations? But not in tipis though right?" These comments highlight just how little we know about this subject in our country. If I'm honest, my knowledge, as you would expect, has increased hugely since our visit. I am happy that I can share these experiences with you.

Just because I'm back home does not mean that the journey is over, in fact it has only just begun. The 'pause' button has not been pressed in any way whatsoever. With the internet and social media, there's a wealth of information at our finger tips. Reuben is always just an email away and through him I have gained numerous Native American friends on Facebook.

I also feel the need to return. There's so much more that I have to see, I need to find out more about the present day. I've become hungry for more knowledge. So, very soon I shall be heading back. Reuben has kindly offered to put me up and introduce me to more influential people, which I'm obviously excited about. In the meantime, there are things that have grabbed my attention that I would like to share with you...

On Facebook recently, I have seen a post that was being 'shared' amongst the Native Americans entitled, 'RACISM...ALIVE AND WELL IN SOUTH DAKOTA', written by Paula Abbott Coome regarding a wrestling competition that her grandson had taken part in. I manage to contact Paula to ask permission to put it in the book and I thank her for allowing me to do so.

So here it is in full...

'RACISM...ALIVE AND WELL IN SOUTH DAKOTA.

My grandson, Nokosi Paul Ringng Shield and his buddy both won 4th place in their respective weight classes at the SDWCA state tournament. I was elated with their accomplishments. Last night I went over to my daughter's home to view Nokosi's matches on track cast. I was horrified to hear commentators make the following comments about my grandson. "Nokosi Ringing Shield, what kind of name is that? He must be straight off the reservation in the hills." And..."look at that ponytail, he looks like a girl." Laughter..."My bet is on the ponytail"...more laughter. Then later one of the men said "all the Native names are long, like sentences." One says something about all of them being poor and having bad habits. One referred to "udders" mooching off the government. Another said "My taxes pay for them." One said "Give me that ponytail. I'll show you what I would do with it." Laughter. My grandson is 6 years old. He is an innocent child. These vile remarks were made by 3 white males working at the South Dakota wrestling tournament in Aberdeen, South Dakota. I am hurt and saddened by the remarks directed at my grandson. I am at a loss at what to do...Sad Grandma.'

As a grandparent myself, I feel deeply for Paula. For the apple of her eye, her young grandson to be subject to such comments by supposedly responsible adults is hurtful beyond belief. The reason that I've raised it here is to show that, quite clearly, not everyone feels the way that I do. I am saddened when I read Paula's post. At this stage of my journey it feels like a slap in the face. How can we ever hope for change? With comments of this type still being uttered so openly, it feels like there's a long way to go before we can start to hope for a better future.

Every cloud has a silver lining, for every negative there is a positive. The response to this Facebook post has been overwhelming. This story has spread like wild fire. The local press and television stations took it on and ran with it. The outrage among both some of the white community and amongst Native Americans was extraordinary. The people responsible for these comments have been banned from taking part in any future events and it would seem that a clear message has been sent out.

This is the sort of reaction you would hope for. The worst thing that could have happened would have been that nobody batted an eyelid, it had not caused a stir and been accepted as the norm. It was not swept under the carpet and that gives me heart.

Unfortunately, these men's regrets will probably be based on the negative effect it has had on their own lives more than how hurtful their comments were to Paula and her family.

Maybe there's an opportunity here to change their views. Perhaps I'm a bit of a fantasist but maybe if people were educated a little on the subject, their opinions would change. If these people were offered the chance to redeem themselves by spending a day or two among the Indians on a reservation along with a few hours in a classroom receiving a short recap of some of the things that they have had to endure through history, they then may see how foolish their comments were. It seems crazy that there can be a racism problem against the people whose land you stole.

An incentive could be introduced to encourage them to take the offer of participating in such a course, a reduction of their ban for example. If they choose not to take up this option, their ban would remain in full.

Since originally writing this, I have subsequently found out that these men were made to do some form of an awareness course, however, from what I've read, this was nothing short of a PR exercise. Apparently two of the men telephoned in anonymously, just known as caller one and caller two. They never had to come face to face with anybody and my guess is that they never learned a thing.

Although, at first glance this may seem similar to my suggestion, in truth it's a million miles away from achieving the objective and is totally incorrect in the way that it has been executed. If this type of thing is going to be effective it needs to be right, otherwise it just adds insult to injury for the victims. Something of real substance needs to be introduced, not just a half-hearted gesture. The question here is, how important do people see this? Building a healthy relationship between both sides is paramount if a better future is to be achieved. Ignorance, among other things, will clearly stand in the way of this happening.

Reuben recently 'tagged' me in a post on Facebook with the slogan 'Every white man should have an Indian friend', obviously this cannot be taken literally but it implies that if we did, we would all have a greater understanding of each other. If only.

CHAPTER SIXTEEN

GENOCIDE?

When the subject of Native America comes up, it's quite common to see or hear the word 'genocide' mentioned, and although it may make us feel uncomfortable, I think it would be good to address the issue rather than avoiding it. Perhaps if we can recognise the bad things that have happened in the past, there could be a way of making a better future.

You may have noticed that in the title of this chapter I have placed a question mark after 'genocide'. Personally, I don't see it as a question, more of a statement. This is just my view and I shall tell you why over the next few paragraphs. If anybody else thinks otherwise, that is their prerogative.

Firstly, let us clarify the legal definition of the word, genocide – 'the crime of destroying or conspiring to destroy a national, ethnic, racial or religious group'.

It is true to say that many Indian lives were lost due to illness and disease that were brought into America by European settlers. As these were alien to the locals, their immune systems were unable to fight the foreign bacteria and germs. As a result, a large number were infected and many perished. For the people that argue against genocide, this is the strongest, if not the only point in their favour. Although there is another side of this argument that suggests that some of these diseases were introduced to the Natives on purpose. Small pox being the main one.

There is however, plenty of information to support the genocide argument. We have already touched on Wounded Knee and you do not need to dig too deep to find other such atrocities. Sand Creek massacre and White Stone massacre to name two more. There are many.

With these events happening over a hundred years ago, it is easy to put them into a box labelled 'history' and say, "well I wasn't around in those days, so it has nothing to do with me." Let me remind everyone that it never ended there. Far more recently, throughout a large part on the 1900's, Indian children were taken from their parents and sent to boarding schools run by Christians. Their hair would be cut short and they were not allowed to speak in their own language. Nor were they allowed to pray to their own spirits. In summary, they were not allowed to be Indians, 'KILL THE INDIAN, SAVE THE MAN', the slogan for these schools.

On my return trip I have arranged a meeting in Denver with Christine McCleave. Christine runs the Boarding School Healing Coalition for people (and their families) that have been affected by this system so is the best placed person to give information on the subject. I'm very much looking forward to meeting her, although expecting some of her stories to be distressing.

On top of the massacres, along with the boarding schools and the killing off of the bison (mentioned in a previous chapter), there is also the issue of thousands of Native American women being sterilised against their will. This occurred as late as the 1970's.

Looking into the atrocities inflicted on these people, it seems that whichever way I turn there is a stone I need to look under. As the list grows to support the genocide argument, another example is brought to my attention, the hanging of 38 Dakota men in 1862, known in short as the 'Dakota 38'. With promised food rations not reaching the Indians, they were going hungry and needed to take some form of action to feed their families. They began to make their feelings known, small battles started breaking out between the Indians and settlers, the military soon got involved, this became known as the 'Dakota Wars'. Seen as an uprising by the U.S Government, 200-300 Indians were rounded up. It resulted in 38 men being hanged.

Recently, in the name of art, without any discussion with the Lakota/Dakota people, a replica of the scaffold gallows from these executions was put up in the grounds of a museum in Minnesota. It feels a little insensitive to say the least and appears to have been taken that way by the Lakota/Dakota people. Another showing of just how little thought and consideration is given to the Native American people regarding these horrific events they have had to endure. I doubt that any malice was intended, at least I would hope not. Perhaps it was done with good intention, even an acknowledgement of the bad past. I'm sure more discussion between the parties could have averted the bad feeling that pursued. Communication has to be the key here.

It's clear that throughout history, to say that times were (and still are) hard for the Natives would be a massive understatement, yet although completely against the odds, the Government didn't always get their own way. The Battle of The Little Big Horn was a prime example. The Native Americans have big hearts and fought valiantly for many years. However, there were occasions when the odds were so stacked against them, they just could not win. There was no way that they could resist the huge tide of people that were taking over their land. The flood of white men was relentless.

I cannot imagine how it must have felt to constantly be on the move, trying to find a safe-haven for their tribe. A place where they would be left alone to live the way they always have, eventually having to give in to the fact that their future lay on a reservation.

I can find no better words than the moving speech given by Chief Joseph of the Nez Perce tribe relating to his surrender to describe how those moments must have felt. In an effort to avoid being placed on a reservation he had attempted, unsuccessfully, to lead his people to Canada.

"Tell General Howard I know his heart. What he told me before, I have it in my heart. I am tired of fighting. Our Chiefs are killed; Looking Glass is dead, Ta Hool Hool Shute is dead. The old men are all

92

dead. It is the young men that say yes or no. He who led on the young men is dead. It is cold and we have no blankets; the little children are freezing to death. My people, some of them, have run away to the hills, and have no blankets, no food. No one knows where they are – perhaps freezing to death. I want to have time to look for my children, and see how many of them I can find. Maybe I shall find them among the dead. Hear me, my Chiefs! I am tired; my heart is sick and sad. From where the sun now stands I will fight no more forever."

Chief Joseph 1877

Every time I read this, it brings a tear to my eye. The hurt and the pain expressed in this short speech is there for us all to see.

These significant times in history have dictated the way life is today for the Native American people. The big question for me is, does it need to continue in the same vain? Maybe the fact that I have fresh eyes looking at the subject means that I see things differently. Both the American people and even some of the Indians to a certain extent have become used to things being this way and are now, to a point, accepting of it.

The past cannot be changed but what stops us making a better future? What could be done to make things that have happened through history a little easier to take? What if the clocks could be fast forward to twenty years from now and things look a whole lot better?

Imagine if Pine Ridge and other reservations were vibrant places. Unrecognisable from the places we see today. Self-sufficient Indian communities. A place where tourists choose to come to embrace the Indian culture. A place where alcoholism is being managed and is in decline. A place where suicide levels are no worse than anywhere else in America. A place where Indian owned businesses are booming. A place where people can see a bright future.

Having given my opinion on my ideal future for the Indians, I realise what I have just done, and I start to question myself. Yes, this book is about 'my' journey and I can get away with adding my views to a certain degree but who am I to tell these people what they need? Does that make me any different from the white men that have planned their future throughout history?

The only thing I can, and maybe should say, is that firstly, some dialogue needs to take place between the two parties to see how best to move forward. Is there any chance of this happening? At this moment in time, I'm not so sure.

END OF PART ONE

Photo opportunity at Devils Tower

Bear Butte stands in the distance

Rattle snake at Reno's Hill

With Rose at the Trading Post

Grizzly and her cub at Yellowstone

PART TWO

CHAPTER SEVENTEEN

THE RETURN

The excitement has been building since I booked the flights for my return. We are now into May 2016 and the countdown over the past couple of weeks for this trip has been the cause of slight contention within my household. Nickey, who I thank whole heartedly for supporting me with this, keeps referring to my return as a 'holiday'! I argue that it's a fact finding, research trip that I would not be going on if I were not writing this book. Nope, she's having none of it, as far as she is concerned it's a holiday, end of conversation. I guess we will just have to agree to disagree on this one.

The day arrives for my departure, Nickey has taken the day off work to take me to the airport. As she drops me off, I hug her and feel sad that she's not coming with me. We say our goodbyes and I head into the terminal.

Over the past week I've been reading about the best ways to get a free upgrade on flights, so I thought I would try all of these little tips to see what happens. Here we go, travel alone, tick. Dress smart/casual, I look down at myself, tick. Do not pre-book your seat, tick. Do not ask for an upgrade, tick. The result, no upgrade and a seat between two strangers with a metal bar from the seat in front blocking where my feet should go. Probably the worst seat on the plane. Next time i'll just pre-book like everyone else. You don't get anything for free in this world.

We touch down in Denver at approximately 5:30pm, I enjoy being able to stretch out and move again. Sitting between two strangers limited my movement somewhat.

As I make my way through immigration, the officer questions me on the purpose of my visit. Why am I here? How long am I staying? How much money do I have with me? Do I have a flight home booked? Thank you for making me feel so welcome!

I collect my luggage and make my way to the bus that will take me to my car rental collection. On this short bus ride, I feel a real sense of unease, "What am I doing here? I've left my family to come here. Nobody is going to want to help me with my book. Why am I even writing it?" I do not enjoy feeling this way, but it is just a case of nerves. I'm alone in a foreign country doing something that I've never done before. I'm completely out of my comfort zone and it affects me a little. I regain my composure and tell myself that things will feel differently in the morning.

So, into the car rental place I go with the words "I am not getting an upgrade" going around in my head. I already have a Ford Escape booked (the same as we had on our previous visit), that would be just fine. However, I would need to hire a satnav. A lady beckons me over from behind a counter. I hand her my booking agreement along with my driving licence. "Could I interest you in an Infinity for an extra $20?" she asks. From past-experience, I'm aware that it is not just an extra $20, it is an extra $20 per day, that's a lot different. "No thank you. I have a Ford Escape, that'll be fine. I do need a satnav though, so how much to hire one of those?" Proud of myself, round one to me. "That would be $12.50 a day but I suppose I could do you the Infinity that has a built-in satnav for $15 a day?" Doh, she got me. Knock out in the second round. "Oh, okay, i'll take the Infinity then."

Not even knowing what this is, I head out to the parking lot to see my car. Parking bay W23, I look up and this beast of a vehicle sits there, almost growling at me. "Do I not need a special licence to drive this thing?" I think to myself. "Don't be silly boy, this is America!!" I answer my own question as I climb up into this monster.

There are buttons and levers everywhere, what they are for I don't have a clue. Fortunately, the actual driving controls are the same as any other vehicle. I start the engine, put it into drive and off I go.

I have a hotel booked close by for this evening and I make my way there. Tomorrow I have a 10am meeting with Christine McCleave in Denver before I head up to Rapid City to stay with Reuben. An exciting week ahead.

CHAPTER EIGHTEEN

THE BOARDING SCHOOL
HEALING COALITION

Well it's official, I hate Denver! Not because it's a horrible place, it is a city like any other, more because of my own driving inadequacies whilst here. The roads are busy and even with the satnav I manage to get lost. It doesn't help that they drive on the other side of the road. The whole thing stresses me out and is not the best preparation for a meeting that I'm already a little nervous of attending. As previously mentioned, I have never written a book before and up until now, this one has kind of written itself but here I am in Denver about to interview somebody, with the sole purpose of gathering information. What will she think of me? I hardly look like an author (whatever that may be like). Will she take me seriously? How should I approach the interview? I decide that the best way is to just be myself and have a conversation with Christine in the same way that I do with clients when I'm trying to find out about their lives, what makes them tick etc.

I arrive at the office building in which Christine works. I head up to the second floor as instructed and inform the receptionists of my appointment. This is a new office block and set out differently to how I imagined it would be. The two receptionists sit side by side, working on laptops, they are just inside the entrance of a modern looking canteen. They smile to greet me, yet because they are not sat behind a traditional style desk, I feel the need to ask if they are receptionists. They smile and nod. One asks who I am here to see, and I give them Christine's name. They invite me to help myself to coffee and say that Christine will be with me shortly.

I'm impressed by the facilities and take up their offer of a drink. There's a self-service kitchen area, and as I start to pour my coffee a voice from behind me says, "Hi Dave." I turn around and see a lady that I assume to be Christine walking towards me. I have painted a picture of Christine in my mind and in it she has the look of a head mistress, as I turn to see her walking towards me I relax a little as she is far less formal looking than in my imagination. My guess is that she is in her mid-thirties. She's wearing a short-sleeved top which exposes a tattoo at the top of her arm. This eases me further as straight away we have something in common. My senses immediately tell me that Christine is the type of person that I'm comfortable around. I get the impression that she is expecting me to be different also, maybe some pompous old Englishman.

The meeting starts a little strangely. I believe that I am here to interview Christine, however, initially it's the other way around. With a pen and paper in front of her, she proceeds to ask me what my plans are whilst here, and with understandable concern, what are my objectives regarding the book? I later learned that I was being vetted. Are my intentions genuine? "Dave, I just need to put my mind at ease, to make sure that you are not just another person looking to exploit the situation that we (Native Americans) find ourselves in?" Christine explains her actions. Fortunately, it didn't take long to convince Christine that I am what I say I am and that there is no hidden agenda.

We soon become relaxed in each other's company and speak openly for almost two hours. We share the same views on many issues and the discussion we have fills me with positivity for the coming days and more importantly, the project as a whole.

Christine is of the Ojibwe tribe and a very inspirational woman with a clear passion for what she does.

Christine's life has been far from plain sailing. She shares with me how she overcame a troubled past involving alcohol and drug abuse that, at the lowest point, saw her lose custody of her son. At that, distressing, heart wrenching time, she realised that she had hit rock bottom. Faced with two choices, Christine could continue to exist in a life that's sole purpose was to feed her habits, or climb out of the hole she had found herself in. This was the moment Christine decided that she had had enough and began to turn her life around. She has now been sober for thirteen years. She knuckled down, got her life back on track and got her son back. Now remarried, Christine also has a young daughter that just the mention of, brings a smile to her face. I have literally just met this lady yet already have the utmost respect for her.

Not only has Christine now got total control of her family life, her career continues to go from strength to strength. She currently sits opposite me in a professional capacity as the focal point of the Boarding School Healing Coalition. The main purpose of which, is to seek acknowledgement of the fact that what happened during the boarding school years is recognised and an apology granted. Yes, this would need to be worded in such a way that the Government could not be sued, yet Canada managed it in 2008, so why not the United States?

Christine tells me that, through the years at these schools, abuse was rife. Unnamed graves are common place in their grounds. Records of events are either hidden or were never kept. It is hard for somebody like me (a person that has never experienced such tragedy) to even try to imagine the pain of the families that lost children with no trace. There are many questions that Christine is looking for the answers to.

There are also a lot of behaviours that are not deemed acceptable in today's society that occur due to things that were learnt through the boarding school years. Physical and sexual abuse being the worst examples. You do not need to have a degree in psychology to know that the behaviour we see and experience as children becomes normal to us and we take on these traits in our own lives. Generation after generation repeat the same patterns. Not only that, it is now believed by some experts that trauma gets passed down through our DNA from generation to generation too. Christine's view is that if an acknowledgement could be made as to what happened in the past being wrong, then people will recognise why they do certain things and then the healing process can begin. It all makes perfect sense. You have to realise that a pattern has been formed in order to break it. It also sits perfectly with my views at the end of part one of this book. To move on from the past, we need to agree that wrong doings occurred.

I ask Christine when and how the boarding school system came into place?

The boarding schools were first introduced under the Indian Civilization Act Fund of March 3rd 1819. This was with the intention of stripping the Indians of their traditions and customs effectively transforming them into Christian farmers or labourers.

Then in 1824 the BIA (Bureau of Indian Affairs) was created, primarily to administer the funds to churches from the Civilization Fund. The BIA still exists today and is in control of the distribution of Government funds that go to Native Americans and the reservations via tribal councils. This may be used to improve roads, schools, hospitals etc. The BIA is still run by white Americans. A lot of Indians may work for the BIA but ultimately, control is still in the hands of white America. Accusations of mishandling of funds and corruption constantly hang like a cloud over this organisation.

The first boarding school to be opened that was not on a reservation was Carlisle, in 1879. Christine tells me that she had recently found out her Great Grandfather was a student there. With our meeting now in full flow, I'm hanging on to every word as she continues with a small piece of her family history. Christine had been asking her Uncle about her Grandfather's Boarding School years at Marty Indian School and Hasky Indian School. When her Uncle sent her a photograph from a family album that also had her Great Grandfather's name, John Wallette, on it, she investigated further. The photograph had the date '1910' on it, so was more than 100 years old. Christine contacted a researcher at Carlisle and was able to obtain her Great Grandfather's records. He had attended the school for 5 years from 1910 to 1915 and had been recruited to play (American) football. Christine tells me, "These dates mean that he played football with the legendary Jim Thorpe!" I am pretty sure, if you are English like me, you are unaware of who Jim Thorpe was. I have looked this up and James Francis Thorpe was a Native American athlete, the first to win an Olympic gold medal for his home country. I now understand the excitement in Christine's voice when she spoke of this. It provides one small positive in a sea of negatives.

Carlisle was open for thirty-nine years and through this time some 12,000 children would be sent there.

To say that I am shocked when Christine informs me that children were still being forcibly sent to boarding schools as late as the 1980's is an understatement!! As I'm a child of the 70's and 80's, it makes it all more real.

Our conversation brings us back to the current day and how Christine is desperately trying to obtain the acknowledgements that she desires whilst President Obama is still in office. Sadly, I know that she was unsuccessful in this. As the inauguration of a new president has occurred during the interim of my visit to the publication of this book (and we all know what happened there), Christine's chances of achieving her goal have become a whole lot tougher. However, I have been impressed with her strength and determination, there is no way that Christine will back down. I only see her becoming more resolute. For what it's worth, she has my support.

To really understand the impact that the boarding school system has had on the Native Americans, I want to share with you some personal accounts of events from these times. I have a Facebook friend that I have gained through my acquaintance with Christine named Jim LaBelle Sr. Jim is a survivor of the boarding school system and can help bring it to life with his recollection of things that he had to go through as a child. I have asked him if he would mind sharing some of his feelings with me and he has been kind enough to do so. Here are a few of his own words of this difficult time in his life…

"As a Boarding School survivor from 1955 to 1965 I experienced fear on many different levels. Fear of beatings. Fear of being shamed. Fearing I would not see my parents if I reported sexual abuse. Fear of not being advanced one grade to the next. Always

110

self-censoring my thoughts and spoken words. Always being hyper vigilant for my safety. Always, always, always. Being met at the home airport by strangers and placed into White foster homes for summers without explanation. I guess you can call this oppression. Somewhere along the line I began to lose the fear and to challenge my oppressors."

Social media can get some bad press at times, yet I have to admit that it has been a great source of information for me. Without it I would never have known of Jim's existence. I have also recently come across another post on Facebook which was originally put on in 2013. It was written by a lady from Saskatoon in Canada, her name is Angelica Jade. I've tried to contact Angelica to gain permission to use her post regarding the boarding schools and how it has affected her life along with the people around her. Sadly, I have not been successful in getting in touch with her. I can see that she has not been on social media for over a year. Primarily, I hope that all is ok with her and it's just a case of her deciding to no longer use this form of communication. It does mean that I cannot use her exact words and will just have to summarise to give you an idea of what was written.

Angelica tells of her step father, a boarding school survivor who is now "killing himself" with alcohol on the streets of Saskatoon. The same streets which took her biological father thirteen years previously. When fuelled by drink her step father would go from being a loveable character to terrifying. She recollects him beating her once for taking a pair of socks without asking him. This stems from his time at school, where if he lost something such as a sock, he would be beaten unconscious.

Her step father also told her that the children in these schools would be made to eat rotten food and if this caused them to vomit, they were forced to eat that too. As he grew older, to protect the younger children, he would eat the rotten food so that they did not have to endure the punishment of what was often the consequence of such an act. He would also give his own items to them if they had lost theirs, so that he would take the beating in their place.

Angelica mentions sexual abuse and gives some details regarding this. Because of the unpleasant nature of these incidents, I shall

111

refrain from being too graphic. However, I will say that this is further confirmation that it was rife in these establishments.

The reason for Angelica's post was to "educate". Sick of hearing people say that they need to stop dwelling on it and just "get over it", she asks the reader to think about whether they would be able to do so if it were them. I will leave that one with you.

During my meeting with Christine we touch on a number of topics. I mention Paula and the racist remarks made about her grandson at the wrestling competition and she highlights a similar occurrence at the ice hockey in Rapid City.

A group of school children from Pine Ridge had taken a trip to the event and it is alleged that they came under racial abuse from people in the VIP section directly above them. They were told to "go back to the reservation" and even had beer thrown on them. It resulted in them having to leave the event early.

Sadly, the outcome of this was not as positive as Paula's case. The main perpetrator was acquitted of a disorderly conduct charge, leaving many disillusioned, claiming that South Dakota is a racist state. Whether this is true or not, these incidents need to be stamped out.

As I work my way through this chapter, a sad, tragic mass shooting takes place in a gay nightclub in Orlando, Florida. Forty-nine people were shot dead and many more were injured. This is a dreadful, horrific story. The news reporter on the screen in front of me relays what happened. She then ends her report claiming this to be the biggest shooting massacre in American history. This story is terrible in its own right, it needs no over dramatization, especially with false claims. It certainly was not the 'biggest', 'worst', 'largest' or any other exaggerated adjective you may choose to use. Not even close…it appears that Wounded Knee, Sandy Creek, White Stone and many more massacres of Native Americans have been deleted from the history books...and right there highlights just how difficult a job Christine has in gaining acknowledgement of the past!

We come to the end of an amazing meeting. I feel privileged to have met Christine and am very grateful of the time that she has spared me. On my arrival, Christine presented me with a Boarding School Healing Coalition tee shirt. I wear this often and with pride.

Before I leave, time for one last question, "If I could grant you one wish for the future of your people, what would it be?"

Her answer, simply, "Healing."

If anyone can achieve this, you are the one Christine.

CHAPTER NINETEEN

RETURN TO RAPID CITY

I leave the meeting with Christine at around 12 noon in very good spirits as I feel that it could not have gone any better. That mood stays with me as I make my way up to Rapid City.

I successfully negotiate my way out of Denver without any problems (which is a relief) and it's not long before I'm on the main highway heading out of town. Reuben is expecting me at about 5pm. To my horror, I look down at the satnav and it's telling me that my journey time is seven and a half hours. This would make my arrival time approximately 7:30. Oops, it appears that I have underestimated the travel time from Denver to Rapid City by some way. This is not good as, firstly, plans have been made for this evening and this is going to put me way behind on timing. I hate being late. Secondly, on little sleep, I now have a seven and a half hour drive and will then be going on a night out.

During the week leading up to my departure, Reuben sent me an invitation via Facebook to a pub crawl in the city for this evening. I very rarely drink and late nights for me nowadays mean going to bed at 11pm because I have been watching something on the television! How am I going to cope?

As the journey progresses, I manage to make up time and get it down to six hours. I arrive in Rapid City at 6pm.

I pull up outside of Reuben's home, he spots me through his open front door and comes outside to greet me. We hug and shake hands as he laughs at the vehicle that I have just arrived in, "I was expecting with you being an Englishman, something a little more conservative, maybe a Ford Focus but you have the biggest Yank mobile I have seen!!"

"Yeah, I know," I reply with an embarrassed smile, "I was determined not to get an upgrade yet ended up driving away in this! I guess, when in Rome…" We walk in through the front door and Reuben's partner, Vivian Billy is just finishing getting ready. Nickey and I briefly met Viv at the Powwow on our previous visit and I've been friends with her on Facebook for a few months, so although we don't know each other well, we are not strangers.

Reuben and Viv share their home with Charlie, Viv's 22-year old son from a previous marriage and Chocco their cat. Throughout my stay I don't see much of Charlie as, like most 22-year olds he is out living life, however, I saw enough of him to know that he's a respectful lad. When introduced to me, he stood up to shake my hand and was always polite when we saw each other. Viv mentioned that he had had a few problems in the past, you would not know it by his current behaviour.

Their home is a two-bed apartment, all set out on one level. As you walk in through the front door you enter the lounge and kitchen/dining area. From the lounge there's a hallway that leads to the bedrooms and bathroom.

After a quick hello, we are back out, in the car and on our way to pick up Darren Thompson, a good friend of Reuben and Viv. Darren, like Christine, is also an Ojibwe and originates from Wisconsin. He's in his early thirties and is currently making waves in the Native American music scene as one of the best North American flute players around at this moment. He is a quiet man and initially I thought that he was a bit shy. The more time that I spent with him, I realised this was not the case. Darren tends to only speak when he has something to say.

We collect him from his home and make our way to the Rapid City Native American Museum where there's a small art/poetry exhibition taking place. Also attending this event is Tate Walker, she is the editor of 'Native People Magazine', a well-respected publication within the Indian community. Darren has recently acquired some freelance work with the magazine writing features on individuals with an interesting story. He will soon be writing an article on Reuben. This is because, outside of being a tour guide, Reuben is also a magician. As far as he's aware, he is the only Lakota in this profession. Reuben entertains at parties and social gatherings. This dovetails perfectly with Viv's work as a face painter. He is also a very good street magician and is a lot of fun to go on a night out with, something I would learn as I spend more time with him.

Tate Walker is exhibiting some poetry, she's a very popular woman and has plenty of people interested in speaking to her. Reuben introduces us and informs her that I'm from England, to which she says in a mocking, posh English tone, "Oh cheerio", we all laugh. I imagine that this is something Tate believes English people say on a regular basis. On hearing my voice, it becomes clear to her that I do not speak in the same way as Hugh Grant and she says, "all I can think of now is the movie 'Snatch'," and it's agreed by all that I sound like Jason Statham.

As Tate is in demand, we only spend a few moments in her company. We do laugh however, at the irony when Reuben tells me that just a few days earlier they were having a conversation about stereotypes and how Indians are perceived by others. Clearly the stereotype that I have been cast in is just a bit of fun, but it goes to show how easily we fall into that trap.

We spend a short while at the exhibition before going along to the first pub on our list. The pub crawl has been organised by the brewery and there are a number of establishments that you must visit and get a card stamped in order to qualify for prizes at the end. We don't get to them all, failing miserably at the challenge set. However, we do succeed in having a good time, which in truth, is all that matters.

We start in a British themed pub (there are a couple of these), and we all order our drinks. Reuben, Viv and Darren all go for British ales, and me? I have a Budweiser!! Real ales are an acquired taste and as I think they taste and look like cold tea, I order a lager.

Although, I do make an effort. The next place we visit is the Fire House, the same bar in which Nickey and I had met the least friendly waiter in America on our last trip, and I have a real ale. A couple of sips in and it's obvious that I'm not enjoying it. The waitress, in complete contrast to her colleague, could not have been nicer. She sees that I am struggling and asks if all is ok? I tell her how I ordered this to try to fit in and the irony of the whole situation. We all laugh (perhaps this waitress gets 'British' humour), she takes the drink and changes it for a lager. I explain to the others that lots of British people do enjoy these beers however, I'm not one of them.

During the course of the evening we visit a number of bars, some with a British theme, others more traditional American style. With yet even more irony, the bar that has the most 'British' feel was not one that was trying to create this. Other than the décor, this pub has a similar atmosphere to that of places back home. We chat with Alex, the friendly barman, while small groups sit talking and others play slot machines behind us. The accents may be different, but the ambiance is the same.

The evening turned out to be a worthwhile one on all fronts. I got to see a lot more of Rapid City, witness Reuben's street magic and the reactions of his unsuspecting audience but best of all, I got to meet people. Some were friends of Reuben, Viv and Darren, others were just strangers.

Meeting new people when you are with Reuben is not a problem, he's a very sociable person and will interact with complete strangers with no encouragement. There are many occasions when he asks me to pick a group of people for him to approach and entertain with a magic trick. He is always well received, and I wonder in my mind how people in England would react to him in similar circumstances. Probably mixed is my guess.

Having given up on the pub crawl, we finish the evening at a bar that is situated on the top floor of the Alex Johnson hotel, one of the tallest buildings in Rapid City. This is a members-only bar. Reuben and Viv have never visited here and are excited at the prospect of doing so. It would be nice to tell you that we are allowed in because of my presence but that would be a lie. We are invited by friends of Darren whom we met a little earlier.

When being introduced by Reuben it is regularly as, "Dave from South-Hampton, he's an English author". Well if you are now reading this in the form of a book, that description will be seen as accurate, however at this moment it feels that there is still a long way to go before I can claim such a thing, I play along anyway.

Reuben knows one of Darren's friends from his school days, this is Ro (short for Arrow) Banks, introduced as the "daughter of Dennis Banks", a well-known Native American activist. Dennis Banks was one of the founder members of AIM (American Indian Movement) and well respected amongst the Lakota people for his work fighting for the rights of the Indians. Sadly, during the course of me writing this book, Dennis Banks passed away. He will not only be missed by Ro, but by the Indian community as a whole.

Ro is with her good friend Red Dawn. When Darren speaks of Red Dawn he tells us that she's a bright lady and will go far. This is proved correct, for at a later date she is voted in as State Senate for District 27, South Dakota at the mid-term elections in 2018.

Ro and Red Dawn are accompanied by a Navajo man that Ro calls her cousin. I'm not sure if they are actually related as it is common for Indians to call close friends 'brother/bro' (Reuben now refers to me in this manner), perhaps 'cuz' falls into this bracket. Well, whether they are blood related is not important, the fact that they get us into the Alex Johnson is.

The Alex Johnson is one of the oldest buildings in Rapid City. There are rumours of hauntings here, specifically on the 8th floor. I can neither confirm nor dismiss this, all I can say is that I never went up to the 8th floor...now some may question my bravery here, but I wasn't scared, no way. The fact that I never left Reuben's side was nothing to do with fear. Of course not...

The lounge area is quiet and relaxed. As we approach the bar, Reuben and I strike up a conversation with a man sat on a bar-stool. He stands out due to his attire. He is wearing a bowler hat, a white shirt and a black waistcoat. His name is Moritz and he raises bison. I think Moritz would make a good poker player as I find it hard to read what he is thinking. He allows us to try on his bowler hat and he may smile once or twice but I'm not totally sure if he is happy or just tolerating us. When I tell him of the purpose of my visit however, we do have a brief yet interesting conversation.

118

As a holistic bison raiser, Moritz occasionally has children visiting his place of work (I assume on school trips) and one thing that he raises with me is his concern at the lack of knowledge the Indian children have on plants and flowers. If there's any difference between them and the American children I do not know as he does not say. I respond to this in the same way that somebody previously had with me when asking why no Indians seized the opportunity to open a small grocery/convenience store amongst the clusters in Pine Ridge, "When you are from a family living on $3000 a year, you tend to focus on survival. Getting through the week, every week. These children may well not have the solid home life that we have and therefore education suffers."

It is difficult for Moritz and I to understand as we do not live on the poverty line. The big question should be, "how can we break the pattern so that in the future these children can learn these things?" I tell Moritz about my earlier meeting with Christine and how she seeks acknowledgement of the past for that very reason. Obviously, that would just be the beginning, but change has to start somewhere.

I explain to Moritz of my interest in finding out what the Native American people would like to happen. What do they see as a realistic resolution? Moritz likes this and says, "This sounds like it will be an interesting book." I hope so Moritz.

I pick up my drink, say goodbye to Moritz and head up a flight of stairs that lead to the rooftop. At the top of the steps, there is a landing that has a couple of tables and a door which takes you outside onto a terraced area. Outside there are more tables, chairs and some open flame fire heaters that have become focal points. They look very decorative but also produce plenty of heat. We stand on the rooftop and look out across Rapid City. It's only a small place, but it has a welcoming feel about it. In a lot of towns and cities in England, on a night out such as this there can sometimes be a bit of an uncomfortable undercurrent. A feeling that trouble is just around the corner. I do not experience that here. What I do experience is a feeling of being on top of the world. As I look down at the city below I'm completely at ease within my surroundings. I'm here with a purpose and I feel good. Although wishing my family were with me, I am amongst friends and it's like I'm meant to be here.

There are not many other people outside. The rest of the party that we came in with are sat at a table just inside the doors. Reuben begins to chat with another Native American man, he is one of just a handful of others out here with us. He's a bit older than we are, maybe about 60. He is very smartly turned out in a burgundy shirt and dark trousers. His long black hair tied in a pony-tail. He is a softly spoken man and I sense that he has his own story but keeps it to himself. I have an inner feeling that he is a widower, although I don't know why. I speak with them both about how I see the Lakota people as a proud race and that through my Native American friends on social media I see how close to their culture they all are. We talk about the Lakota language and I comment that I never see it fading into extinction because too many people care. The youngsters will grow up knowing how important their heritage is and make a conscious effort to keep it alive. He thanks me for my acknowledgements of his people and tells me that he believes my book will be a success. I thank him in return. As I leave him, I think to myself what a nice man he is.

Reuben and I venture back inside and sit on a bench a few feet away from the others. By now we are somewhat inebriated and chatting freely. We speak about certain words that may be used more in England than in America, more specifically, swear words. I am informed by my good friend that there is only one word that he finds truly offensive and if he ever heard anyone calling Viv this, he would flip. This word is 'Squaw'. I am aware that this word is incredibly offensive to Native Americans as when we were with Rose on our previous visit, I mentioned that I had not heard the word spoken on my trip. It was made quite clear to me that this word is derogatory and should not be used. I took on board what was said but explained to both Rose and now Reuben that if you hear an English person saying it, please do not take offense as it is being used in ignorance. Our understanding of the word is that it means female Native American. Since I found out the feelings regarding this, when I now hear it said it has the same effect on me as the 'n' word when talking about Affro-Carribeans. It makes me feel uncomfortable. The good thing is, now I know how offensive it is, I can tell others and they will hopefully refrain from using it too.

The evening draws to a close at around 1:45 and we wait at the front of the Alex Johnston with groups of other people for taxis to come and take us home. Reuben entertains with more tricks as we wait.

Tonight, I have drank way more alcohol than I'm used to, I'm still in control but also in very good spirits. As the taxi delivers us safely back at Reuben and Viv's, I am grateful for a wonderful night but also relieved that I made it through.

I'm asleep very soon after my head hits the pillow.

CHAPTER TWENTY

THE MORNING AFTER

Ouch!!

I wake up just a couple of hours after falling asleep. My head is pounding. A reminder that my body is not used to this. I'm tired, still under the influence of alcohol and very dehydrated. There's a bottle of water at the side of my bed that I placed there in preparation for this moment, yet I cannot muster the strength to get it. My head is so heavy, impossible to lift. I lay here attempting to go back to sleep, but my head is too painful. This continues for a couple of hours. Eventually, I dig deep, lean to one side, reach down and grab my water bottle. I sip it like I have been stuck in the desert for a week.

I ask myself how people do this on a regular basis and reassure my body that it will not be happening again for a very long time.

I drift off into broken snoozes before dragging myself out of bed between 9:30 and 10. I can hear others talking and moving around as I make my way from the bedroom that my hosts have kindly given up for me.

My body feels very weak and fragile. As I walk into the lounge, a part of me is happy to see Reuben and Viv suffering in a similar way, not because I enjoy seeing them suffer, more because they will not be expecting a lot from me in the day ahead.

Reuben offers me a coffee and some food. I know this is exactly what I need even if it may be tough to get down. I have a coffee with sugar, I usually have it without but need the energy. Reuben also cooks me an omelette which I eat in very small mouthfuls, each one a struggle. It is a relief that Reuben is my host and a good one at that. Looking after myself may have been too much of an effort at this moment.

With croaky voices we speak about the night before but with long pauses in between sentences. These are not uncomfortable silences, more a reflection of how delicate we all feel.

After eating I go outside to telephone Nickey to let her know that all is okay and to check all is fine at home. I tell her how rough I feel, and she laughs. "You know you don't drink," she reminds me. "I have no plans on making it a habit neither!" I say with some conviction. Our conversation is short and sweet. I will call again later when I feel a little better.

As I return to the lounge, Viv decides that she will go for a sleep and heads to the bedroom. Reuben and I sit talking and relaxing as the recovery process takes place.

A couple of hours pass, Viv returns and we all get a bit of colour back in our cheeks. We discuss our plans for the rest of the day and Viv says that she will cook a Mexican pork dish for dinner. It would be mine and Reuben's job to go and get the ingredients needed from the shop.

Darren is doing a talk/short concert at the museum at 5:30pm and we had said that we would try to get down to see him. Sadly, the day passes us by and we do not get there. However, Darren, with Ro, Red Dawn and 'cuz' come to visit after his show. You can tell that the adrenalin is still pumping through Darren when they come in. The performance had gone well, he is in high spirit.

They share the meal with us that Viv has cooked, and it is agreed by all that she has done a good job. As we eat, Reuben speaks a little of what he does. He follows this up with some more of his magic tricks, each one leaving us confused as to how he has done it. Reuben also talks of how he sees his life, living with one foot in the

123

Native world and the other in modern day America. The others nod in agreement.

I think this is a perfect description. I cannot begin to tell you how difficult this must be. Over the coming week especially, and throughout the course of my journey, I would not go as far as saying that I have one foot in each world but most certainly stuck a toe in to get a feel. Although I am enjoying every second of it, it's not as easy as you may think. You question a lot of things. Arguments take place in your mind regularly. I have tried to be clear on the things that are in these pages yet, if occasionally they come across a little muddled or even contradictory, I can only apologise but it is for the reason that I have just mentioned.

I am aware that the people I'm in the company of this evening have interesting lives yet with the mood being one of light heartedness, it does not seem like the right time to start asking questions and effectively interviewing them. I also find myself going into my shell a little, not completely, but I'm not quite my usual self. Being in a minority of one is a strange feeling. There is no hostility towards me, nothing but friendship yet I find my guard going up. I become aware of everything I say and do. I'm not uncomfortable but certainly not fully relaxed.

I get the impression that their Navajo friend was feeling in a similar way as he was even more quiet than I. He is from out of State and works in construction. I am from England, work as a Personal Trainer and am writing a book. Not much more was shared by either of us.

Fortunately, the others are outgoing people and keep the conversation flowing. Ro and Red Dawn enjoy life to the full and there is a lot of laughter as they speak.

The night comes to an end. Our visitors leave, and I make my way to bed. Tomorrow will be a busier day, although today was just what the doctor ordered. Nothing too strenuous for my delicate, hung over body.

CHAPTER TWENTY-ONE

ROAD TRIP TO STANDING ROCK

On occasions during my trip I would step back to consciously take in where I am and what is going on around me, to not let the moment pass me by. It's easy to be swallowed up by your surroundings and to fail to see how far you are from your normal, everyday life. This Sunday morning is one of those times. As I sit in the armchair in the lounge, Viv is getting her travel bag ready for our road trip to the Standing Rock Reservation in North Dakota. Reuben's (biological) brother Carlos, who lives on Standing Rock, is set to take part in a Sundance next month. As it is his first time doing this, in the next couple of days he will be partaking in a preparation ceremony that has him spend 24 hours alone up on 'the hill' (a hill close by that is used for these ceremonies). He will have to stay within the boundaries of a small rectangular area and is not allowed any form of unnatural lighting nor will he have any purpose-built shelter, although as I understand it he can take a tarpaulin to lay under should the weather turn bad. It is just him and whatever nature throws his way. This is a big deal and I'm privileged that I will get to meet Carlos just prior to this major, spiritual event in his life.

Reuben is preparing eagle feathers at the kitchen table. He is making a fan out of one of the wings for Carlos to take up with him. You may be wondering how these eagle feathers/wings were acquired. Did we go out early this morning to catch one? Fear not, even if we had the inclination, the hunting of eagles in America is illegal. These birds are protected and have to be applied for. This can only be done by Native Americans. Applications are made to the Wildlife and Fisheries Committee and when dead birds are found they are sent out to the people that have requested them. The whole bird is packed into a box with polystyrene for protection and sent through the post. Reuben and Viv on this occasion have received a spotted eagle, which apparently just means that it was still young. This bird had one good wing which Reuben was using but the other was damaged and the obvious cause of its death. I sit and watch as Reuben attaches a leather hand grip to the base of the wing in order to turn it into a beautiful fan.

The eagle, an impressive creature, is sacred to Native Americans and treated with respect. Although I'm sad that this wonderful bird had died, at least it had died of natural causes. The fact that the feathers would be used in a positive way, somehow makes up a little for the premature death of this particular young bird.

As I sit watching I think about how surreal this is, yet it is the reason I'm here, to experience a totally different culture first hand. A Sunday morning like no other. The beauty of it is, this is not a show put on for the tourists, this is being done for a real reason and would have been done if I was sat here or not.

Although Reuben and Viv are just like me in so many ways, we laugh at the same things and get mad at the same things too, this is an example of how we are from two different cultures.

Once Reuben has finished, we turn our attention to getting ready for our trip to Standing Rock.

Being registered to a Lakota/Dakota, Navajo, Mohawk or Haida reservation, gives free reign to live on any within those tribes and still receive health care and food. So, although Reuben went to school and grew up on Pine Ridge, he is a Hunkpapa and therefore registered to the Standing Rock Reservation.

This is also the place where the great Sitting Bull had once lived, albeit against his will.

Darren has decided to come along with us and use the opportunity to promote his music, more so, his latest CD. It will be his first visit to Standing Rock too. I have a large enough vehicle. The more the merrier as far as I'm concerned.

It is a four to five-hour drive from Rapid City yet there's no rush, we are working on American Indian time, we will get there when we get there.

Although it might be some distance between Rapid City and Standing Rock, there are a lot of connections between Reuben and Viv with the reservation. As I have already mentioned, Reuben's brother lives there but also Viv's ex-husband and younger son reside there too. Charlie has an ex-girlfriend that has moved back there also, we shall be returning some of her things whilst there. Darren has a female friend, Samantha, living there, with whom he shall be staying. These are just a few of the links, it is clear that the Native American community is a close knit one.

We load up the wagon with our travel bags, the things that we are returning to Charlie's ex, the eagle feathers (placed with care), a case of water for the journey and before we even get anything of Darren's in, it already looks like I have hired the right vehicle.

We pick Darren up at lunchtime and add his travel bag and flutes to the back of the Infinity. We decide to eat before we get on the road to North Dakota so make a final pitstop at a drive-in burger bar.

Eventually, we set off. The drive from Rapid City to Standing Rock is an enjoyable one. I make use of our time on the road by chatting further with Darren to find out a little more about his story. I know that he is from Wisconsin and is a professional North American flute player but what brought him to Rapid City and what got him into playing the flute in the first place?

As previously stated, Darren is an Ojibwe. He tells me that it can be written or pronounced as Ojibwa (with an 'a' – O-jib-wah) or Ojibwe (with an 'e' – O-jib-weh) or even Chippewa. The last example is said this way because the French used to have problems pronouncing the 'O' at the beginning. I have seen this written in each of these forms, it's a little confusing and I am glad that he cleared it up.

Darren moved to Rapid City in 2014 when he was offered a job working on the production team for a Scottish director who was making a movie on Pine Ridge, 'Neither Wolf Nor Dog', based on the award winning book by Kent Nerburn. This premiered in Edinburgh in 2016. The filming took eight weeks. During this time Darren met a girl and when the job finished he decided to stick around. The relationship never progressed, and they split shortly after. However, by now Darren had grown fond of the Black Hills and his life in Rapid City so stayed on regardless. He was beginning to gain recognition for his music and picking up some good contracts. He now plays regularly at the Crazy Horse monument that Nickey and I had visited on our previous trip. He is winning awards frequently and has other well-respected musicians looking to work with him. During our time at Standing Rock he sells a number of CD's to retailers.

I am fascinated to hear how Darren became interested in this instrument in particular. Whilst studying for exams at the age of nineteen he was looking for a way to relax, to take away some of the stress associated with such times. As he sat watching the movie 'The Lord of The Rings', he felt himself drawn to a piece of pipe music that was playing on the screen. This led him to a similar sounding North American flute and the work of Raymond Carlos Nakai, a Navajo/Ute who started playing this instrument in the 1980's, continuing successfully to the present day. Such is the power of music, it evoked memories of Darren's childhood. He then looked closer at the instrument and was fascinated by stories from elders talking of the trees singing. At first Darren never understood quite what they meant, but he later realised that the trees do sing, they sing through the beautiful flutes carved from their wood. He began to teach himself to play. It soon became apparent that Darren had a natural ability to produce wonderful sounds with this instrument and is now able to do this professionally. He does not just play notes, he plays stories.

At the end of our chat, we put on Darren's latest CD. We spend some time relaxing to this peaceful music, eating up the miles as we drive through the open plains of the Dakotas.

About halfway through the journey we stop a short toilet/bathroom break and to give Reuben and Viv a chance to smoke their pipes. I cannot recall seeing anybody smoking a pipe since my father did back in the 70's, until this trip. It doesn't seem odd in anyway, probably because they are both a little eccentric, it suits them.

Back on the road, we continue into North Dakota and Standing Rock. A short distance into the reservation we stop outside the home of an uncle of Reuben's so that he can give him an eagle feather that he has asked for. The rest of us wait in the car as Reuben runs his errand. When news gets around that somebody has an eagle, it is quite common for the person in possession to receive requests for a feather or two. These will then be passed on to those that have earnt them.

Continuing-on, we head towards the casino/hotel that we plan to spend the night. On our way we cross the Missouri River and enter a different time zone. This is a new experience for me. I have crossed different time zones on many occasions, but it has always been in an aeroplane, this is the first time that I have driven through one. I don't reset my watch and just have to remember that it's an hour out every time I look at it.

Before crossing the river, we pay a visit to Sitting Bull's burial site, well one of them at least. There are two places that claim to have the remains of the great man, over the next few days we visit the other site too, just to make sure. For some reason, I strongly believe that the place we visit first is the actual site. It just feels right.

We park the car and walk the short distance to the monument erected in Sitting Bull's honour. It is a quiet location away from everything. We pay our respects in our own way, Darren plays some music as we stand looking at the statue and out across the Missouri River. The Lakota translation of Sitting Bull's name is Tatanka Iyotaka, which literally means bull that sits. He is a hero to all four of us, so we savour our moment at this spot. Sitting Bull lived from 1831 to 1890 when he was killed by one of his own people that worked for the Indian agency police as they attempted to arrest him, believing that he was involved in the Ghost Dance that would also lead to the Wounded Knee massacre just a couple of weeks later. "I wish to be remembered as the last man to hand over his rifle," one of Sitting Bull's famous quotes. So that is exactly how I think of him today whilst standing here, close to where I believe he lays.

Within the same area there is a plaque put up in memory of Sakakawea. Sakakawea was from the Lemhi Shoshoni tribe and was the wife of a French trapper named Charbonneau, they were employed by Lewis and Clark for their expedition of all things west of the Missouri River to the coast of the Pacific Ocean. Little was known of this part of America prior to this expedition which took place between May 1804 and September 1806, commissioned by the president at the time, Thomas Jefferson. Charbonneau and Sakakawea were taken along because they could speak Shoshoni. Sakakawea was invaluable to this project for her ability to communicate with the native tribes that they encountered.

It is nice to see that some recognition has been given for her contribution.

Outside of the U.S, we tend to hear of Christopher Columbus and his 'discovery' of America. Less is known about Lewis and Clark, who effectively opened-up the west of the country for white settlers to move into. Hard to believe that this never happened until as late as 1804.

We leave the Sitting Bull burial site and make our way to a casino close by, this is where Reuben, Viv and I plan to stay the night. Unfortunately, there is no room at the Inn for these weary travellers. Okay, so it is not an Inn and we are not particularly 'weary' but whichever way you look at it, they have no room. The helpful young man on reception allows us to use his telephone so that we can book something a little further down the road in a town called Mobridge. Reuben and Viv had lived in this town for a while a few years ago so know the area.

They book us into a hotel close by and tell me that it has a nice bar/restaurant overlooking the river. Sadly, the bar at the hotel is closed, as is the restaurant, so our dinner would need to be sourced elsewhere. There is a restaurant just a two-minute walk along the road that would serve our purpose. Darren remains with us for dinner, he has arranged for Samantha to pick him up once we have finished. We have a drink in the bar before heading to a table to eat. A nice steak and a beer is a good way to end a long day.

We part company with Darren for the evening and head back to our room. We lay on our beds, the TV is showing a music awards show at which Celine Dion delivers her acceptance speech in French while Adele, via a video link, accepts hers in English. I laugh the following morning when two disc-jockeys on local radio speak of the awards, joking that they understood more of what Celine Dion had said than Adele.

We fall asleep watching the television.

CHAPTER TWENTY-TWO

LADONNA

"Morning Reuben, are you aware that you have sleep apnia?" These are the first words that I utter on this day which may tell you a bit about the night sleep that I had. I say this tongue in cheek, I am being a little unfair. I had slept fine until about 4am but once awake, Reuben's ailment became very evident. Viv, with her earplugs and blindfold seemed to sleep well enough, clearly a seasoned pro when it comes to sharing a room with Reuben. For those that are unaware, sleep apnia is a disorder in which you stop breathing whilst asleep. This shocks your body into waking up, you then start breathing again and continue with your sleep. From the moment I woke, I witnessed this about every ten minutes. Reuben is used to it, it has just become a part of his life. So, the answer to my question is, "Yes, I have had it for years."

I have a shower, feel refreshed and ready for the day ahead. Well, at least after breakfast I do. Reuben and I are both big on eating first thing. Viv skips breakfast this morning.

We check out of the hotel and make our way back into Standing Rock. Shortly after entering the reservation we make a quick stop so that Viv can say hi to her younger son, John. We pull off the main road and into a residential estate. Reuben and I wait in the car on this occasion, however, I do get to meet Viv's son and ex-husband a little later on our trip. After a few valuable mother/son moments, Viv returns, we leave the estate and return to the main road. I use the term 'main road' but only because it is fast moving, it is not particularly busy. As we turn right on to it we enter a stretch of the road named after another of Viv's sons that was tragically hit by a car and killed at the age of four. Although a number of years have passed since this happened, as you would expect, it is still very tough for Viv to deal with. When she tells me of this tragedy, I struggle to find words of comfort. I wish that I could say something that would make a difference, but I can't. I listen and show remorse. My heart is sad for her and all concerned. Life can be cruel.

Reuben has been in touch with Darren and arranged to meet him outside of the Tribal Office. We make one more stop on our way there, paying a quick visit to Carlos so that Reuben can give him his eagle fan and to see how he is feeling ahead of his twenty-four hours on the hill that will begin the following day. We arrive at his home, the children are playing in the front garden. Reuben knocks on the door and Carlos's wife answers and invites us in. Carlos is sitting at the dining table preparing prayer ties ready for his big event. After being introduced, I ask him how he is feeling? Is he ready? He seems to be in good spirit and tells me that he just needs to sort the last couple of things and then will be good to go. Reuben presents the fan made from the eagle wing and Carlos smiles and looks at it affectionately. In his eyes, you can see that he loves this gift as he thanks Reuben warmly. It was worth the effort that Reuben had put in.

Carlos works at the Prairie Casino on the reservation, which is where Reuben, Viv and I will be spending the night. He reminds me of a younger version of the Native American man that Reuben and I had spoken with on the rooftop of the Alex Johnson a couple of days prior. He also has long black hair that he wears in a pony-tail, this is obviously not out of the ordinary amongst Native American men. Carlos speaks with a soft voice too. He has a calmness about him that is infectious, an aura that is welcoming and I feel at ease in his presence. Our visit is a short one, but we tell Carlos that we will see him again before he goes up on the hill. For now, it is goodbye as we have a meeting booked with Ladonna BraveBull Allard at the Tribal Council Office.

We meet Darren in the carpark across the road from the office building. He is waiting for us when we arrive. In the carpark stands a strange statue, it looks just like a boulder mounted on a brick pillar. It is believed that this was a woman or child that turned to stone. This is from where Standing Rock sourced its name.

We enter the building together and are greeted by Ladonna. Very occasionally throughout our lives we meet people that have a lasting effect. People that command an instant respect. This is most definitely one of those times. The next thirty minutes or so will live with me forever.

Ladonna is a very well-known and respected member of the Tribal Council and is regarded as one of the most knowledgeable historians on Standing Rock. I believe she would sit comfortably at the top of any business in America. She also has a look to match, a mature lady with strong features and a sharp dress sense.

Today, Ladonna has a white Englishman sat opposite her that is writing about his journey into her culture. There is no way that this lady is going to allow me to walk into her office and leave unmoved. I tell her that my aim is to 'scratch the surface' of this subject, to give as many people a little insight as I can. She replies, "I do not do 'scratching the surface'". As I sit across the desk from her, she looks me in the eye and asks, "So what do you know?" followed by a couple of simple questions that any Native would know the answer to. I do not however, but I'm sure that this is her intention. "You don't know?" Ladonna mocks me a little, I think she is having fun. A case of her setting the boundary, a way of saying, "you are not one of us, you will never feel the pain we feel". This is all done with a soft voice and a smile, which only increases my nervousness. At this point I begin to feel as though I have been thrown into the lion's den. I laugh and tell Ladonna to, "Stop it, you're scaring me." She smiles, I can sense her pleasure at this, she has achieved her goal. She is in control. Thankfully she takes it a bit easier on me from here on in.

I have made it clear throughout my story that I am just an Englishman on a journey. I make no claims to having Indian blood, I have never professed to be an expert on American history. I'm just an everyday guy experiencing something special. In fairness to

Ladonna, she has probably encountered many people that claim to understand the plight of the Native Americans through what they have been fed by the media along with the version of history taught in U.S schools. I respect this, but hope that she will quickly realise that I'm not one of those people.

After laying down the tone of our meeting, Ladonna begins to tell me some things of interest regarding her culture. She talks of the different bands within the tribes. As I understand it there are three bands of Sioux; Lakota, Dakota and Nakota (Nakota are Canada based). Each band are made up of a number of smaller tribes. Standing Rock has people from both Dakota and Lakota, although mostly Hunkpapa, Lakota live here.

Ladonna speaks proudly as she tells of her people's understanding of nature and how scientific they are, explaining that they know how the wild turnip, one of the first crops to grow in Spring, carries all the nutrients the body needs to recover from the winter months. Continuing with the nature theme, Ladonna talks of how important the herb 'sage' is to the Indian people. Yes, they use it to smudge, but it has far more uses than this. Ladonna believes it to be one of the best detergents around. She says that if you boil it, you can use the water for all sorts of cleansing tasks, from wiping down work surfaces in your kitchen to your skin if you have a poor complexion.

She then turns to talking of a major topic that is on everybody's lips at the moment, the Dakota Pipeline. There is a protest camp set up on Ladonna's land down at the Cannonball River to oppose this oil pipeline. I believe that this has raised the fighter spirit within her. This is stirring inside and the reaction towards me is evidence of this. Ladonna gives us directions so that we can pay the camp a visit the following day, to offer support and to find out a little more about it.

As we briefly discuss this, Ladonna tells me, "This generation of my people will save the world." I find this a bold statement and I question her, "You believe that this generation will save the world?" She looks straight back at me and says, "I do not believe, I know," with an unmoving conviction.

The seriousness of our conversation builds with each sentence as Ladonna talks of the oppression of her people and the horrendous way in which they have been treated throughout history. She mentions a similar discussion she had previously had with a white

American man, during which he asked, "so what could be done to make things better?" Ladonna's response pulled no punches, her next line cut through me like a knife. Her answer, "How about you let us kill *your* children". At that moment, and only when she spun it on its head did it really hit me, WE-KILLED-THEIR-CHILDREN. As I write this, tears are forming in my eyes. We killed their children. The true realisation hits me as hard as anything I can ever remember.

Ladonna then expresses to us that in the past she never believed that trauma could be passed on through generations, until she visited the site of the White Stone Massacre. This is where her Great, Great Grandmother, at the age of 9 was shot in the hip. She survived and was taken by soldiers and placed in a prisoner of war camp. As she recollects her feelings from her visit, Ladonna's voice begins to tremor, tears well up in her eyes and start to roll down her cheeks. This woman's strength is unquestionable, yet I am now also seeing her emotional side. I see sadness, but most of all I see passion. As she looks across her desk, I reflect her emotion with a similar expression. I may not be able to share in her grief, but I can share in her sadness and also her anger. I try to hold back the tears, well I'm a man after all, but inside I am overcome with Ladonna's pain and feel a strong sense of guilt. With Reuben, Viv and Darren the only other people sat at Ladonna's desk, I feel as though I have become a representative of the White Race and right now, I am anything but proud. I want to apologise but somehow me saying the word "sorry" is not going to cut it. One thing that is truly evident here is the fire that burns inside this lady. I will take away a lot from my time with Ladonna, the most significant of which; the purpose of my journey, which has now increased hugely.

Our meeting comes to an end. I want to give Ladonna a hug. In most emotional situations this would be normal, here however, it would not have been appropriate. I shake her hand and thank her for her time.

This inspirational woman may have given me just a few moments out of her busy day, but this meeting will be imbedded in me for as long as I am alive, and I thank her for that.

As we leave Ladonna and make our way out of the office building, I visit the bathroom to wash my face and gather my thoughts. I lean across the sink and look at my reflection in the mirror, the cold-water runs down my face, off-of my chin and into the basin below. Eyes still red, I puff out my cheeks and exhale slowly through closed lips. I feel a little emotionally bruised yet grateful of the experience.

Once outside I make a call home as I know that with the time difference, Nickey will now be back from work. It is hard to express to her what has just happened, her day has been the same as any other. However, it's good to hear her voice and how things are at home. As much as she moans about me, apparently I'm being missed, which is nice to know.

I hang up the phone and now feel ready to continue with my day.

CHAPTER TWENTY-THREE

SITTING BULL COLLEGE

Our next stop is to be Sitting Bull College. This is seen more as an opportunity for Darren as the college hold a concert once a year that he is interested in taking part in. They also have a shop that he may be able to sell some CD's to. For me, everywhere we go and everyone we meet creates a chance of learning something new. I'm more than happy to visit.

Reuben and Viv have both been students here in the past so are familiar with the place and the people that work here. We enter the building, Reuben and Darren wander off to see if they can find anyone to help us, Viv and I hang around in the library.

The walls of the library are decorated with black and white photographs which hold my attention for a moment but the most impressive thing, in a glass case, is Sitting Bull's headdress. There is a notice at the top of the glass forbidding any photographs being taken. I must admit I am a bit disappointed by this, I would love a picture. Viv tells me that I should take one anyway as there is no-one around. I respond with, "...but Viv, as soon as I put it on social media or even in the book, I could get caught out." She laughs, "I didn't think of that, I guess that's why I'm always getting into trouble." I nod and laugh along with her.

Reuben and Darren return, they couldn't find anyone, however, shortly after Mark Holman appears. He is the Library Director here at the college. Viv and Reuben know Mark well and are pleased to see him.

Mark is non-Native. Earlier I wrote of stereotypes, one that many have is of American men being loud, brash and boastful. Once again, a stereotype has been shattered as this could not be further from the truth when talking about Mark Holman. He is polite, welcoming, very unassuming and a pleasure to be in the company of.

Darren speaks to Mark regarding the concert and manages to secure a place performing at the next show. He also sells some of his CD's to the shop here. Already the visit has been a success.

For me, as I stated before, this is just another opportunity to sit and have a conversation with somebody that has an interesting story. So, how did Mark end up on a reservation working at Sitting Bull College? I ask him about his story and although happy to speak, he looks a little perplexed as to why anybody would want to know.

Mark grew up on a farm in the eastern part of North Dakota. In 2001, at the age of 31 he moved to Bismarck, a large town within the state, with his girlfriend. He got a job at the college on Standing Rock and has stayed ever since.

Something that I'm interested to find out is, how was he received as a white man when he first arrived? As an outsider, did he have to win people's trust before he was properly accepted?

I put this to him, this is his response;

"I think I was pretty well received from the start, but as with any community, people open up as they get to know you. The main thing was the learning curve for someone who 'just fell off the wasichu (non-Indian) truck' as I like to say. A play on an American idiom about falling off a turnip truck as someone who knows nothing. Learning how things work on the rez (reservation). Standing Rock is a complex place where the diversity of the tribe reflects that of America without clear visible lines between white/non-Indians and Indians except as people define them individually. When I first came to Standing Rock, some of the people I thought were non-Indians

139

turned out to be Indians and some of the people that I thought were Indians turned out to be non-Indians."

Mark's comments indicate that life on the 'rez' is never straight forward. The description Reuben gave earlier on my trip of having one foot in each world is clearly also experienced by Mark, yet from the other side.

I hope that Mark writes his own book some-day. I would certainly read it.

Our conversation turns towards the college. Founded in 1973 it has between 250-350 students of all ages, ranging from very young (the language immersion nest has children as young as 3) to people in their 70's. The majority of which are from Standing Rock. There are a large-number of subjects taught, such as nursing, teacher education and business. As you would expect they have Native American studies, Lakota/Dakota languages, environment science and social work. Add to that, programmes on truck driving, electrical, construction and welding and you can see that there is enough of a variety to fill most people's needs.

Mark suggests that we head over to the Lakota language nest, telling Reuben and Viv that other mutual friends that teach there will be around and would love to see them. We take his advice and pay the immersion centre a visit. This ends up being one of the highlights of my trip.

We say goodbye to Mark and make our way over to where these classes are held. Just one last thing before we go, "Would it be okay if I take a photo of Sitting Bull's headdress?" I ask cheekily. "Yeah, sure. We only have the sign up so that we can keep track of who does so," he answers. See, I told you he's a nice guy.

We enter the building where the young children are taught the Lakota language and make our way along the corridor to one of the classrooms. Reuben points to a sign on the door and laughs. The sign reads 'NO ENGLISH'. Fortunately, this is not a nationality ban, but a ban of the English language. I am free to enter, as long as I keep my mouth shut. The children are taught that, whilst in the classroom, they must only speak Lakota.

A lot of the children's parents do not speak Lakota, so, when at home, they may well only communicate in English, effectively making it their first language. Some of the parents make an effort to learn Lakota too, so they can aid their children's progress.

As we enter the classroom I'm very conscious not to speak. The teacher, Ti Tolman, is an old friend of Reuben's, and they greet each other in a way that you would expect, at least I think they do as I can't understand a word they are saying.

Reuben introduces us to the class, I nod and smile. Darren speaks a few words in his native Ojibwe tongue. He then proceeds to play a short piece of music to them.

Reuben then takes to the floor and performs some magic tricks. I manage to keep up with what is going on throughout as there is plenty of animated pointing and signing.

Viv and I sit on tiny children's chairs and watch the joy on the youngsters faces as Reuben reveals the surprise elements within his tricks. There are about ten children aged 5 to 6 years old, every one of them deeply engrossed in Reuben's performance.

Witnessing young children enjoying themselves the way that they clearly are here is always special but knowing what I do regarding the concerns of the continuation of the language and how the future of the Lakota culture relies on this type of education, this classroom becomes a place of such importance.

You could argue that the future lies within the children of every community, and rightly so, yet here, this is increased greatly.

We are all wearing big smiles as we leave the classroom. It has been a very uplifting experience visiting the college, but most of all the Immersion Nest. I personally feel privileged to have been able to see the future first hand. A big well done to Ti and his wife Tipi, whom I also met briefly, for the amazing work that they are doing.

As we make our way back to the car, we comment how cute these kids are and how much we had enjoyed our time in their presence, especially Viv.

It is now early afternoon and we decide to make our way to Prairie Casino to book a room for the night. The casino sits on the top of a hill surrounded by open plains. At the booking-desk we reserve a room for Viv, Reuben and I, Darren is once again staying with his friend Samantha. Reuben mentions his brother Carlos to the lady serving us and we can see from her reaction that he is a popular member of the staff.

Our room will not be ready for a couple of hours, so we have a wander around the casino before taking a seat and making it a base point for a while. We sit in the comfortable chairs drinking complimentary coffee. Darren disappears for a spell and returns to tell us that he has just "donated" $30 to the casino via a slot machine.

Carlos has now started his shift and we see him for a few moments whilst he does his rounds. Reuben tells him of our meeting with Ladonna and he asks how it went? I smile and say, "It was actually pretty difficult. Ladonna is a tough lady eh?" Carlos's response, I believe, sums up the type of person he is. In his soft voice he says, "Don't let anyone make you feel bad." On this evidence, Carlos has the knack of saying exactly the right thing at the right time. It's nice for me to hear those words at this moment.

While we wait to get into our room, Reuben attempts to contact his good friend Dakota GoodHouse. I have exchanged a few emails with Dakota (I mention him in a previous chapter), he lives in Bismarck and we thought that it would be great, as we are close by, to meet up in person.

After a few attempts, Reuben eventually gets through and we arrange to meet in a pizza restaurant in town. Viv is feeling a little tired and decides to sit this one out, preferring to rest up. It has already been a long day.

After unloading the bags from the car and settling into our room, we leave Viv watching television and venture off to meet Dakota. It takes us an hour to get to Bismarck. The town is busy, yet we manage to find the restaurant and are lucky to find a parking space close by.

We arrive a short while before Dakota, go in and order a drink while we wait. A soft drink for me as I am driving, the usual beers for the other two. Dakota arrives moments later and joins us at our table. He orders a soft drink too as he is teetotal.

Having communicated with Dakota a couple of times via email, it is great for me to meet him in person, to put a face to a name.

The restaurant is an independent establishment, the pizzas are freshly made and cooked in a clay oven. This is normally a sign that they will be good...and they are.

We make general chit chat for a while, telling Dakota what we have been doing over the past couple of days. This is the first time that Darren and Dakota have met too, so a little of introducing themselves follows. They talk of mutual acquaintances that also play the North American flute along with some elders within the Lakota community.

Dakota mentions a winter count that he is currently working on. Unaware of what a 'winter count' is, I ask him to explain.

A winter count is a yearly, chronological account of events throughout history, done through pictures or symbols. In the past, these were done on bison hide but over time, with the demise of the population of these animals, they have taken to more commonly using canvas.

It works to a system where a significant event will represent a certain year. For example, if it was based on modern day Britain, 2012 may have the Olympic rings and 2016 could have something to do with Brexit, a major thing for which that year will be remembered. The year in which you wish to start the winter count is at the centre of the piece and the following years work outwards in a spiral formation.

Dakota tells us that he is working on two at the moment and that they are in the "trunk" of his car. He would be more than happy to show them to us. There is a park close by that we could head to where he could open them out for us to see. Once we finish our pizzas, we head back to our vehicles and follow Dakota, driving up the road to a recreational area situated close by. We park up directly behind Dakota's car, beside a small grassed area within a residential estate. The houses that surround it look quite large and I'm of the assumption that this is a more affluent part of the city. There is a beautiful, very large statue of a flying eagle carved out of wood which grabs my attention as we walk from the car. There's also a band stand that we settle just in front of.

Dakota pulls the winter counts out of the bin bags in which they are stored and unravels them onto the grass. One is a bison hide, the other is canvas. The canvas one unrolls to about 2-3 metres in length and has a lot of pictures and symbols on it. The types of things on this particular winter count are; the Space Shuttle launching, rain and lightning (which represent a year which suffered bad floods), basketball team victories, things that are seen by the prospective owners as significant.

The bison hide has not long been started and only has fifteen or so pictures. This is a work in progress that Dakota is putting together for a customer.

I think to myself that it would be good to create one of my life. I smile as I wonder what year will be represented by the eventual publication of this book.

Our time with Dakota GoodHouse comes to an end. I'm very happy that I got to meet him in person. It has been a very enjoyable couple of hours.

We also leave Darren behind as Samantha is picking him up once again.

As we leave the city and get back out into the open plains, I look in my rear-view mirror and as the sun sets, there's a bright orange sky behind us. In complete contrast, ahead the sky is very dark. During our drive, I witness the most fantastic lightning storm I have ever seen. The sky is alive with so many forks of bright light that flash over the open land, like the flicking on and off of a light switch. This is a show that would overshadow any rock/pop concert. Some believe that this type of extreme weather is Wakan Tanka (the creator) sending a message. After my meeting with Ladonna earlier today and a scheduled visit to the Camp of the Sacred Stone tomorrow, this could certainly be interpreted in this way tonight.

As we drive we can see the lights from the casino elevated in the distance. The rain is not yet upon us, although we can see it heading our way across the plains. It becomes a race to see if we can make it back to our base before it reaches us. We fail. The heavens open above, the wipers on the Infinity are working at maximum speed yet I can still barely see the road. My vision is so impaired, I slow down to a snail's pace.

We creep along the road towards the casino, the rain falls as heavily as if we are driving under Niagara Falls. My thoughts turn to Carlos and how fortunate it is that he's not going up on the hill until tomorrow. That said, I'm sure that some other poor soul will be up there tonight. The experience of facing up to the elements in such a way must be invigorating, however, given the choice, a warm, dry night would suit me better.

We arrive back at the casino and head up to the room to check that Viv is okay. She has comfortably settled in for the night. A little nightcap down at the bar for Reuben and I puts the finishing touches to a day that has had me on an emotional rollercoaster. A ride that I will never forget.

CHAPTER TWENTY-FOUR

I STAND WITH STANDING ROCK

After a similar night sleep to the one I had yesterday, I'm awake early yet again. Reuben continues in the same pattern of waking up every 10 minutes or so and then going straight back off to sleep. My mind immediately switches back to the previous day and our meeting with Ladonna. I begin to write down some notes, not so much of what she had said but more of the way that I felt. It is important that I get something down on paper while the powerful impression that she has left on me is fresh in my mind.

An hour or two pass before Viv and Reuben begin to stir and then wake up. We potter around for thirty or so minutes preparing for our day ahead.

Once ready, Reuben and I go down to have our breakfast. The restaurant is empty except for a small group of maybe four or five people congregated at another table. The waitress comes over to take our order and we have the usual set of questions...how do you like your eggs? What coffee would you like?

As we wait for our breakfast to arrive, Reuben receives a message from Darren saying that he will not be able to make today as something has come up. He has also sourced an alternative plan to get back to Rapid City a few days later. This is a shame as it means I will not get to say goodbye in person, I will have left to go home before he gets back to South Dakota.

We eat breakfast then collect our stuff (and Viv) from the room and check out of the casino. We set off to the camp, on our way we make a very brief stop to drop off the clothes to Charlie's ex-girlfriend. Viv exchanges a few pleasantries with the girl's mother and then returns to the car. We are now travelling one person and a whole load of baggage lighter.

As we get closer to the camp, we turn off-of the tarmacked road and onto a dirt track. The camp comes into view along-side the Cannon Ball River. There is a tipi set up to the left, away from another ten or so smaller tents. We leave the car in a convenient spot and walk into the camp. There is a large-sized fire burning with chairs placed around it, some occupied and some empty. It sits a few feet away from a large tent that is set up as a canteen/kitchen area.

I am sure that at some point you would have read or seen something, either through a news feed or on social media regarding the Dakota Pipeline and the mass demonstrations by the people of Standing Rock along with their supporters to prevent this going ahead. At the start of my journey, I never expected that the biggest thing in modern Native American history was going to happen right in the middle of it. Today I get to visit, in its very early stages, the site where the people are beginning to make a stand, The Camp of the Sacred Stone.

At this moment, there are maybe just 20 - 30 people here. Over the coming months this will grow to between 10 – 15,000. The best way that I can describe how important this has become is to tell you that it is the first time since The Battle of The Little Big Horn that all seven bands of the Lakota Nation have come together. As the movement grew, it became an accumalation of smaller camps that together made one big camp. The main one named 'Oceti Sakowin', which means the seven fires burning.

We meet and speak to a few of the people here. Understandably, they are reluctant to give their names. They do not know me and therefore do not trust me, why would they? However, they are happy to point out in the distance, across the Cannon Ball River, the machinery of the workers that will be drilling under the rivers.

At present, there are no real plans by the protestors, no strategy as to how they are going to tackle this force that is heading their way. They know they need to be here, they have to do something, answers will unfold as events take place.

There is an old Lakota prophecy that tells of a black snake that makes its way across their land and destroys everything in its path, effectively bringing an end to mankind. The Lakota people see this oil pipeline as the 'black snake' and have even named it as such.

I have read that the original plan was for the pipeline to run under the Missouri River close to Bismarck. This was found to be un-desirable to the people of this city, so was redirected to go under the Missouri and Cannonball Rivers a little way up-stream from Standing Rock. It would also be going straight through Indian burial grounds and treaty lands. The deepest concern to the people on the reservation is the high percentage chance that this pipeline will leak, and their water will be contaminated. During my conversation with Ladonna, she had told me that the type of oil that would be transported is very abrasive and made a point of saying that, "it's not a case of IF it leaks, it is more a case of WHEN."

As I write this, a lot of time has passed since my visit and an awful lot has happened. I have tried to follow what has been going on through various Facebook groups and friends that have been closely linked. Viv and Darren have been very active and spent a lot of time at the camp, Reuben has also spent some time there but not as much as the others. Although the movement has his full support, it's not so much his thing to be on the front line.

Being in the fortunate position of having friends that were heavily involved, I do not pass up the opportunity to ask about their experiences of their time spent at camp. Viv's account of things really paints a vivid picture of how it was and what it meant to the people.

I sent Viv a message asking a few basic questions such as, how long was she there? Why she felt the need to be there? What was it like? And so on. Her response…

"I was at camp periodically from the time of our first visit which we made together Dave, until I began living there on a permanent basis in September and that is where I stayed until the final evacuation in February.

It was important for me personally to be there as my children were raised there and one of my grandchildren lives there in McLaughlin. My son John, who you met Dave, lives in Kenel, and as you also know my youngest, Baby Frank is buried there along the river.

I have lived on Standing Rock on and off for twenty years. It's a place that I frequently call home.

It was a major importance for me to be there, to put it all on the line for my children and future generations. This was a common feeling amongst the water protectors."

I ask Viv how her time there has affected her?

"The time I spent there still bewilders and amazes me. It hurts even now. I sometimes wake up crying after dreaming of being there."

I'm aware that many suffer with P.T.S.D (Post Traumatic Stress Disorder) from their time at camp, Viv is clearly one of those. That said, there's still an overwhelming sense of pride and joy regarding what they achieved. This is summed up in Viv's next paragraph…

"So many miracles happened. I witnessed the stuff of legends, was in the presence of greatness. To be surrounded by people who are awake and conscious on this scale is unimaginable, awe inspiring."

Viv points out, however, that it was "no vacation".

"EVERYDAY we were on the frontline, halting construction with our Non-Violent Direct Action. EVERYDAY we had ceremony, walking in sacred space and being mindful of all the spirits and ancestors we involved. We attended daily camp meetings along with training, whilst also doing our fair share of the work."

I pick up on the 'training' comment and ask Viv to elaborate a little.

"NVDA (Non-Violent Direct Action) was constantly promoted amongst the people. It was vital, the essence of how we would carry out our actions."

So, although the authorities would have us believe otherwise, Viv makes it clear that every attempt was made to ensure peaceful protest through NVDA and prayer.

It is common-practice in this type of dispute, to discredit protestors to try to turn public opinion against them in any way possible. This appears to be the case here.

"I wasn't officially affiliated with any camp... I served as a community resource and liaison between Camp Leaders, Tribal Leaders, local tribal members and new coming people. I was everywhere and did a bit of everything, never idle."

Aware that Viv had been arrested during one of the protests, I ask if she would mind sharing this experience with me.

"On October 27th, I was arrested during the North Camp (a.k.a Treaty 1851 Camp) raid. We stood our ground there as the 'No Surrender' line. It was the entrance to the east side of HWY 1806, on UNCEDED TREATY LAND that is part of the original territorial boundary identified in the 1851 Treaty. It was taken by imminent domain and NEVER given up by the Lakota. So, we invoked Treaty 1851 by occupying it to protect the waters being threatened by this pipeline.

Even though DAPL had purchased it, it had been done so illegally...the land was not zoned for commercial ownership, only pasture and grazing.

After being sprayed by tear gas, shot at by law enforcement officers and assaulted, we were illegally arrested and effectively kidnapped by law enforcement.

There were 141 of us arrested and carted off to jails around North Dakota. It was two days before our people even knew who was locked up. We were only identified by the numbers they wrote on our arms...my number was '134', I believe that means 134 of total arrested to date.

On day 4, from Devil Lake County Jail, some of us were bussed back to camp after being bonded out for the sum of $1500, due to be charged with a felony.

All 141 of us were charged with Felony, Engaging in a Riot, Mis-demeaner Endangering by Fire or Explosion and Mis-demeaner

Maintaining a Public Nuissance. At our Preliminary Hearing, all felony charges were dropped.

Under the advisement of The Water Protector Legal Collective, and in court Solidity, most of us told the judge that we did not recognise the authority of the court, at which time she put our pleas to 'Not Guilty'...which actually gives the court jurisdiction. On July 13th 2017, my charges were dropped, the day before my trial.

For now, I just want to say that my heart is heavy with the memories and experiences we all shared as a family."

I am very grateful to Viv for sharing this.

I also contacted Joye Braun, a lady that was there 24/7 throughout the campaign. A stalwart of the whole movement. She continues with her work promoting 'Mni Wiconi' which translated means, 'water is life', taking on the big money oil-companies. Joye, is a proud Lakota lady. She has the maximum 5,000 Facebook friends from around the world and was a good source of information throughout this conflict.

Unfortunately, Joye's perception of people such as myself (outsiders writing books, articles, tv shows etc) has hit an all-time low. Exploitation of her people has become a problem yet again. I am grateful that Joye at least read my message when I contacted her. Originally, she agreed to give me her account of events as all profits are going to Indian charities. I sent, by her request, written confirmation that this is (and has always been) my intention. Joye also wished to know "which charities?" In-fact her response to my first message was very brief, just those two words.

I declared my desire to make 'The Boarding School Healing Coalition' one, and stated that, having visited the 'Immersion Nest' at Sitting Bull College, I would be happy for that to be my second choice. With fifty percent going to each. Joye, has close relations with Tipi Tolman at the college and confirmed that this would be a popular choice for her.

For me, these two charities are perfect. One to address the past and the other to address the future.

Unfortunately, although I contacted Joye a few times to chase this up, she never actually sent it over. Perhaps there are trust issues, maybe she has just been too busy. Whatever the reason, in my opinion it is sadly an opportunity missed to reach out to the other parts of the World, although I totally understand and respect her decision.

This whole movement was an amazing time for the people. They stood together in solidarity against all the animosity thrown their way. From security dogs being set on them to being sprayed with ice-cold water in sub-zero temperatures. They remained as immoveable objects. Yet all these negatives created a positive.

I recently asked Darren if he could comment on his time at camp and for his reflection on his experiences there?

"My time at the camps in Standing Rock were some of the most impactful experiences I have ever had. It was a time of love, respect, dedication as well as sadness. Sad to see the camps that inspired peoples from all over the world, come to an end. There may never be a time like that again and, frankly, there shouldn't be." Darren's words may be few, but they are very much to the point.

The protesting of the pipeline and the protection of the water was big enough in its own right yet for me this movement was way more than that. It was the Native Americans standing up and saying, 'enough is enough!'. 'You have to stop treating us as second-class citizens.' All the years of oppression came to the surface.

On a personal level, from the comfort of my everyday life, as events at the camp unfold, I watch in horror on my computer. I feel helpless. I share the videos on social media to try to raise awareness. I buy an official 'I STAND WITH STANDING ROCK' t-shirt. I email Amnesty International (I know that they have people at the camp) to ask what they are doing to stop the poor treatment of these people. They tell me to sign their petition. "I am sick of signing petitions! I have signed numerous petitions and nothing changes," my latest little outburst goes unanswered. The term, 'the world is watching' is banded around but, that is all we are doing, watching. I contact a local MP to ask whom I should write to regarding this, no response. Way back, directly after my first trip to Pine Ridge, before I even started writing, I emailed President Obama regarding the treatment of these people, no response. I have come to the conclusion, that other than the likes of you and I, nobody cares. The powers that be certainly do not, that's for sure. Perhaps if we keep talking about it, sooner or later somebody will have to listen.

The camp came to an end when Trump, in his first two weeks in office signed off the job, giving permission for the drilling to continue, something that Obama had not done. The previous president had halted the work, waiting for more tests to be carried out regarding the affects this could have to wildlife in the area. Although, many strongly feel that he could have done more.

The Water Protectors were given an eviction notice and had to be clear from the site by the date stated in February 2017.

In June 2017 the drilling under the rivers began.

In an earlier chapter I raised the question of what may be acceptable in a modern world to the Indian people so that a brighter future can be strived for. Well I think I have the answer as to where it should start and that is with respect. Until we respect these people and their rights we will get nowhere.

Back to my visit, we roam around and chat with the guys here and offer words of encouragement. More magic tricks from Reuben to help keep spirits up. Viv tells them to remain strong. You could see the fire in Viv's eyes even at this early stage. It's not a shock to me that she went on to play a strong part in the movement.

I can now say, looking back, what an amazing achievement it was for these people. The tiny camp at which I stood, became huge. A massive story of worldwide interest was developing beyond anything I could have imagined. I think back to the words of Ladonna, "This generation of my people will save the world." I cannot and would not argue with that.

Our time here comes to an end, we want to catch up with Carlos before he heads up on the hill.

As previously mentioned, my regrets are few from my journey but one more I have is, that I never got to visit the camp when it was in full flow. Maybe it was not meant to be. Perhaps it is important that my view is from the outside looking in, that my perception remains objective. Although, it sounds like it was a very special time.

"Good luck guys, stay strong." We raise our hands to wave farewell as we leave.

CHAPTER TWENTY-FIVE

A BIG DAY FOR CARLOS

Reuben's phone rings as we pull away from the camp. It is Carlos. He is calling to ask if we would be able to pick him up along the road as his ride could only take him halfway to the base from where he will be going up on the hill. Reuben relays his message to me. "Of course, just give me the directions," I answer.

We meet Carlos by the side of the road just after a junction. He's waiting by the car of his initial ride. He transfers his gear from one vehicle to the other. We are now back to almost fully loaded.

I am directed off-of the main road once again and onto a tougher terrain. We drive on grass, along dirt tracks, through divots, up and down hills. The rain from the night before has dried up so at least it's not muddy, although it still feels as if I have taken a four-wheel drive experience. All of it is effortless for the Infinity.

We come to a clearing in an otherwise wooded area, this is where the base camp is situated. There are a few tipis erected and a fire burning. There's also something that resembles a den, maybe four feet high with a thick tarpaulin over the top. This is the sweat lodge. When the participants come back down from their twenty-four hours on the hill, they spend some time in there to encourage visions.

When we pull up, there's no one around. We climb out of the car and within a couple of minutes two men arrive in a pick-up truck. These are the organisers. They shake our hands and make light conversation. The guy that seems to be in charge tells us that he saw Reuben and I this morning at breakfast. He was one of the group at the other table. I guess we stick out a little and that makes us easy to remember.

He tells us that he is a Crow. As appears to be the norm, mutual friends and acquaintances are mentioned. I actually feel a part of the conversation on this occasion as they mention Curtis RealBird, with whom I went on the ride-out at the Little Big Horn on my previous visit. Reuben points this out and I tell them how much I had enjoyed my short-time with him.

Carlos looks as though he's taking it all in his stride. If he is nervous in any way, it's not evident. I think that's just his way. They run through a check list of everything that he should need to take up with him. He has most of it. Reuben and Viv offer for us to drive to the shop to get the couple of things that are missing. Carlos is not fussed but we do so anyway. The nearest shop is a forty-five-minute round trip away. It is a convenience store that stands alone on the highway. A little reminder of how vast this country is and how far away from everything we are.

We get back and spend some last valuable moments with Carlos. The other three have a smoke and we offer words of support. He's still showing no sign of nerves and is looking forward to getting on with it. With only a short-time left before he heads off, we leave him to gather his thoughts. I shake his hand, wish him well and thank him for allowing me to share these moments. He smiles and thanks me in return. Reuben and Viv both hug him. You can see the pride in Reuben's eyes as he says goodbye. The next twenty-four hours are big in the life of Carlos.

It later becomes apparent how sensitive these events are when Reuben wishes Carlos well on Facebook and urges everyone to have him in their thoughts. Another Native American makes a comment stating that this is a spiritual ceremony and should not be put on social media. Reuben responds by saying that he has placed no details and that it's just a case of supporting his brother. He is a little upset by the criticism and asks Viv and I what we think. With social media being a relatively new thing it's difficult to say what the correct protocol should be. Viv and I don't see that he has done anything wrong. However, it is an example of a traditional culture struggling within a modern world. I like to take the view that there's always a chance you could upset somebody, but as long as you have goodness in your heart, you can do or say these things with a clear conscience.

Back on the road. We pay one last visit to the Immersion Nest at Sitting Bull College so that Reuben can perform some more magic tricks to the children that were not involved yesterday. They watch with joy just as the others had. Led by Ti Tolman, they sing a Lakota song to Reuben as a thank you. There's a good atmosphere around this place and I enjoy being here, however, we have disrupted their classroom for long enough and it's time to say goodbye. We leave Tipi, Ti and their staff to calm down a lot of excited children. Oops, sorry.

We hear from Darren once more and he invites us to pop by his friend Samantha's house on our way back to Rapid City. She lives a couple of doors up from Carlos, so we know exactly where to go. We only spend twenty minutes or so here as we still have the long drive back to contend with. We are invited in and see Darren is in the kitchen cooking. We speak about our visit to the Camp of The Sacred Stone and of seeing Carlos before his event. Darren tells us about his day which he had spent with his friend and her children. It was nice to be able to say goodbye to Darren in person. I have enjoyed my time with him. I have also enjoyed hearing him playing his music. North American flute playing on tap can be highly recommended.

Time to head back to Rapid City, well almost.

Viv asks if we mind stopping off to see her son again on our way. Of course not. We pull up outside of her ex-husband and sons house. Her ex, Frank, invites us to sit with him. Frank is a stout man with shoulder length, black wavy hair. We sit chatting on the wooden porch of Franks home. It is the end property on his road. There is a similar house directly opposite, to our left there is waste land and woods.

Frank works for the Tribal Council and is also a very keen photographer. He shows me some of his camera work which is amazing. One picture in-particular stands out to me, it's of rolling clouds that resemble the ocean. It's a mesmerizing, beautiful photograph. He takes his art very seriously and will go out at all hours to capture a perfect scene.

Viv and Frank are amicable to each other, although you can sense that there is no love lost between them.

Our conversation turns to events unfolding at the camp regarding the oil pipeline. The people we had spoken to there had told us they believe there is in the region of half a million dollars put aside by the Tribal Council to fight this. They were hoping that some funds would be made available to them for food/water supplies.

I mentioned previously that at the camp I could see a passion in Viv's eyes, it became evident to me quite early that Viv has a fighter spirit burning inside and that this whole DAPL business was stirring her. She mentions the half a million-dollar pot to Frank, and suggests that some funds should be made available to the water protectors. Frank sees it a little differently. He tells us that the protestors will need to be self-sufficient. Yes, there is money put to one side, although he would not confirm that it was half a million, but this would be needed elsewhere. "If you are taking on a multi-billion-dollar oil company, the pot that you talk of does not last long. It will be swallowed up pretty quickly in legal fees." A very good point and one that I had not thought of.

Remember, that at this moment the protest is just a handful of people down at Cannon Ball River. It feels a little strange looking back at some of the issues we were discussing knowing how it turned out.

Frank is a no-nonsense kind of guy and isn't shy in giving his view. I like this. As with the majority of people that I have met on my journey, I feel as though we got on well. I know that may come across a little boring, but it genuinely has been the case.

Frank is of the belief that, not just at camp but in general, more Native people should be self-sufficient.

Many of the people that I have met throughout my journey, like Frank, are keen to see a change in attitude that would improve the future of their people. A break away from the past as such. To hold on to the things from their culture, like the language for example but to drive them forward in a positive way. There are a lot however, that

157

do not share their attitude. Some are of the impression that they are owed. Their lands have been stolen and the treaties broken, end of story. It is difficult to argue against that, as we know that it's true, however, that attitude does not bode well for a brighter future.

I get the impression that, working for the Tribal Council, Frank is on the end of people requesting funds daily. Some worthwhile causes, some not so. It's probably a little draining.

The difference in attitudes obviously causes divides amongst the people. They are aware that this is a problem as they use the term 'divide and conquer' on a regular basis when they explain their current position.

Perhaps the coming together of so many to fight the black snake can unite them more in the future. As Viv and Darren told us, this was a very positive experience. I hope that its legacy lives on for decades to come.

One thing that has become apparent to me, is Native Americans are, by tradition, a generous race of people. When we use the term, 'kind to a fault' maybe this could be said of them. Perhaps it has contributed to their downfall. However, I hate saying that, as it is a beautiful trait that sets them apart from the rest and one of which they should be proud.

It is common, when visiting Indians, for them to give you a gift. The t-shirt from Christine is a prime example. Before we left Frank's house, he said, "I have something for you," and went inside and brought out a box with a mug that has the tribe emblem printed on it, he also gave me some sage. These gifts are very special to me. Sadly, I could not bring the sage home because of custom laws but the mug is used regularly.

Viv gives her son John one last hug before we leave them to continue with their evening.

The grave of Viv's younger son is only a minute or two up the road, we stop off so that she can spend a few moments there too. Reuben and I sit quietly in the car as Viv walks over to where baby Frank rests. She returns a little while later wiping her cheeks. She shows me a photograph, a fresh faced young boy looks at the camera. I say how cute he looks and that she must be proud.

There is a respectful moment of silence as we pull back onto the road that will return us to Rapid City.

We drive back through more rain and storms. We are not too far into our journey when darkness falls. When we get a dry moment, we stop briefly so that Reuben and Viv can smoke their pipes. Whilst stopped, Viv pulls a small velvet pouch out of her bag that contains a tiny amount of sage. She places it on the dashboard of the car, this is to aid our safe trip through the bad-weather.

The radio plays songs from the 80's as we drive the final stretch. Reuben, Viv and I are all-of a similar age. This music is from our era, we all sing along as we go.

It is about 11pm when we arrive back in the city. The streets are quiet. A young lad, probably about 14 years of age walks along the road alone, "What's this guy doing out at this time?" Viv asks. They tell me that there is a curfew for youngsters under the age of sixteen. They are not allowed out between the hours of 10:30pm to 5:00am from Sunday to Friday and 11:30pm to 5:00am on Fridays and Saturdays. As it is the middle of the week, this young guy is clearly in breach of the curfew. He does not appear to be in distress or in any trouble, so we leave him be. Hopefully he will make it home before the police catch up with him.

As I am just a visitor to the city, it is difficult for me to say if this curfew is worth having. I can only relate it to how I think it would work back home and I'm not so sure that there is a problem with youngsters being out between the hours stated. For a short while in the past, I did a little casual youth work which involved a young lady and I walking around the streets of local estates. This was between the hours of 7pm and 9pm. Our role was to be a face for the youngsters to chat to. We would ask them how school is going, are they attending youth club this week etc? Just a friendly adult face for them to interact with. Maybe this soft approach is better, maybe not. Perhaps somewhere between the two could be the answer. Questions for another day.

We arrive back at Reuben and Viv's home. It has been a busy few days, followed by a long drive. We are all very tired. We sit, have a drink and relax to unwind from our time on the road. We speak about Carlos up on the hill and hope that all is going well.

The last few days have had me in a bit of a whirlwind. So much has happened. I have visited some places of real significance and met some amazing people. I'm under no illusions as to how fortunate I am. There is also no doubt in my mind, that if it were not for my brilliant hosts, none of this would have happened. I really appreciate what they have done for me.

Totally shattered, I head to bed. Only one more full day left with these wonderful people.

CHAPTER TWENTY-SIX

ACCEPTANCE

Today we will be going back to Pine Ridge. It is a day of running errands and visiting other members of Reuben's family.

We wake up at our leisure as we are under no time constraints. There's a nice relaxed mood this morning. Reuben had placed a lot of pressure on himself to help me gain as much information as he could during our trip to Standing Rock. Now that part was over and had been successful, he could settle down and just enjoy our last full day together.

Whilst having our breakfast, a parcel arrives. Viv opens the box and says with a little excitement, "Reuben, it's your new hat."

This is the first day of a new-look for Reuben. I am already aware that he is fond of hats, the arrival of this parcel cements that. Inside the box there is a black top hat. Reuben takes it out and tries it on, it fits perfectly. He decorates it with 'steam punk' glasses and a couple of small feathers. His straight, black, shoulder length hair hangs from the bottom of it. It looks 'different' yet pretty cool.

Reuben likes 'different'. He has also now taken to wearing a long black cape along with the hat. This most certainly is a break from the ordinary.

We leave home late morning. Viv and Reuben need to pop to the bank in Rapid City before we make our way to Pine Ridge, plus I need fuel for the car.

We visit the bank first, Viv and I wait in the car. A lady inside complements Reuben on his headwear. He is smiling as he tells us, he is clearly happy. We then stop for fuel and are now ready to head out of town. As we leave the gas station, Reuben says something that takes me aback. He and Viv tell me that they would like to adopt Nickey and I as Lakotas.

Wow!

I could never have imagined that we would get to this point. When I set off on my journey, I would never have thought that it would come this far. It had never even entered my mind. I am aware that Nickey and I got on really well, firstly with Reuben on our initial visit, now also with Viv on my return. We have become close. I never realised quite how close.

It would require a proper ceremony, giving us an excuse to return. Any reason to come back is welcomed by us, for a reason as significant as this, even more so.

This is amazing and if it were to happen, I would be honoured, as would Nickey. However, if it were not to happen, it would not be a problem and would not dampen my excitement of the original offer. The reason is simple; acceptance. The people that I have spent the most time with, Reuben and Viv, totally trust me and know that I am genuine. That fills me with pride. Today, I'm a very happy man.

Positivity breeds positivity. As we drive towards Pine Ridge, Viv receives a business call. A booking for both her and Reuben's services. It's turning into a good day for us all.

On we drive, through familiar territory (it was just six months ago that I was last here), it is all fresh in my memory. Back into the Badlands and beyond.

When writing of my first visit to Pine Ridge, I mentioned how important it is to look at things through fresh eyes. Well, my eyes are no longer as 'fresh' as they were the first time around and the shock factor has gone. My impression this time is that it's not as bad as I remember. A case of familiarisation breeds contempt maybe. It is easy to see how things are accepted as the norm.

This time I manage to see a bit more of Red Cloud School, for on this occasion it is open. With all of the shootings that happen in schools across America, I'm amazed that we can just walk freely into the building. Three strangers just strolling straight into the sports hall without being challenged. I'm not so sure that this would happen in schools off the reservations.

There is a group of students inside the hall that appear to just be hanging out in here, they do not give us a second glance. Perhaps the confidence that I have gained over my time here makes me a bit more inconspicuous, you tend to carry yourself in a different way when you are comfortable in your surroundings. Although being a white man does make me stand out a little. Not only am I white, I'm naturally very fair skinned (it's common for white people to comment on how pale I am!). My behaviour does not draw attention and I get to see things in a more natural setting.

Having not been able to gain entry on our previous visit, it is nice that Reuben now has the chance to show me around. He points out a large board that is fixed to the wall with the names of record holders of different running distances. He shows me where his name appears, twice. One for the 400 meters, the other for the 800 meters. It also shows the times that were achieved, 51.8 for the 400m and 202.3 for the 800m, they are the sort of times that I would associate with professionals. These have not been beaten by any student since he set them in the mid 80's, I am impressed. Reuben was some runner. For a part of his early life running was a big focus.

"As a youngster I used to run for pleasure. It was my way of getting away from the reality of life on the rez, kind of an escapism I guess.

I would head off to the hills and just run. All of these miles paid off and my times on the track reflected that.

As I got into my early teens, I decided to have a go at a triathlon that was happening in Hawaii. I'm not the best swimmer and had never swam in the sea before, so that was never going to be my strong event. On my way there, I spent a couple of weeks with Billy Mills, the Native American Olympian. He assisted with my training and was a great inspiration.

On the cycling section I had a nasty crash, so that, along with my poor swimming, affected my position. It also made me realise that triathlons are not for me.

I carried on with the running for a couple more years but as I got a little older my passion for it began to fade and over time I done it less and less until I stopped completely."

Reuben does not appear to have any regrets, "It's just the way life panned out".

We have a little wander around the school and visit the small shop that is located just inside the main building. I buy a translation book for Lakota/English. It's not very thick but has a few phrases and some commonly used words. I love the language and how it sounds. I learn some basics, Hihunne waste, Dave Jones emachiyape – good morning, my name is Dave Jones. Philamayaye – thank you. That said, most of my pronunciations are probably nothing like they should be.

From Red Cloud School, we make our way to the Tribal Council Office as Viv and Reuben need to apply for their entertainment licences. These will give them the official documentation needed to carry out their professions on the streets as well as at social functions.

There is a significant difference between the Tribal Council Office at Pine Ridge and the one on Standing Rock. The Standing Rock office is a newer building. It is more open, light, airy and welcoming. The Pine Ridge one has the feel of a DHSS office back in the UK. It is dull, miserable and a little depressing. The people that work here reflect the decor. The man that serves Viv and Reuben is abrupt, bordering on rude. There is very little eye contact and only a few words spoken, he gives the bare minimum in response to questions asked. It gets me wondering, why the difference? Is it to do with the different-types of attitude that I mentioned after our chat with Frank. Maybe, it is a case of their surroundings affecting their mood? This could be said of Pine Ridge as a whole not just the Tribal Office. On the other hand, it might just be a bad day and I am over analysing.

Most of Reuben's family live on Pine Ridge, with the exception of Carlos, obviously. Whilst here we visit his sister Lisa's home. His brother Joe, Joe's wife and Mavis, Reuben's mother, are all here.

Lisa is at work. She is a nurse. There are a number of children here also, some are Joe's and some are Lisa's, they are all playing in and out of the house. It's refreshing to see young children playing outside, a rarity these days.

Reuben introduces me, "Dave from South-Hampton, an English author", here we go again. Another embarrassed smile forms on my face. He tells them that he and Viv wish to adopt me and that I will be a new member of the family. That feels a little strange, being introduced in such a way. I hold the embarrassed smile.

Joe is a big guy with short hair. His wife Marion is cooking fry bread (Indian tacos). Mavis sits at the dining table facing the kitchen. Joe comments on Reuben's new hat and mocks him a little. He admits after that he really likes it. They have a fun relationship and rib each other in what I see as a 'British' way. Native American humour is very similar to ours and a little different from American humour in general. They say mean things to each other in the same way that we do, all tongue in cheek and with no malice, just for comical effect. The new hat is an opportunity that Joe cannot pass up.

Mavis is a lovely lady in her seventies. Although maturing in years and a little frail looking, she has the heart of a lion. Mavis speaks quietly, a trait that Carlos must have inherited from her. Amazed that I am here all the way from England, she asks how long it took me to fly here? She then asks if my parents are still around. I tell her that they are, and she smiles. Mavis tells me of her younger days and how she loved to sing. She also used to ride the horses at rodeos. You know the event where they race around the oil drums? She had to quit doing this after continuously cutting her legs on the sharp edges that would jut out from the drums. Getting as tight as possible into the turns is needed to get the quickest time but the jagged edges cause nasty lacerations to the rider's knees. Mavis tells me that she was a bit of a tom boy in her younger days, a tough cookie. I believe her.

She insists that I have some fry bread and asks Marion to bring me some. It's freshly cooked, still warm and tastes lovely. It's very filling, and I feel bad that I cannot eat all of it.

Joe, keeping up with the Native American tradition, brings me a gift. A crucifix made out of beads by the creative Marion, I thank them. I love the hospitality that these people give. I could not have felt anymore welcome.

The only one of Reuben's family left for me to meet is Lisa, his sister. As she is working today, I feel that it will not happen, on this occasion at least. Reuben has other ideas. Our next stop will be the hospital.

Fortunately, when we arrive Lisa is not too busy, and we manage to say hi and have a brief chat. I find out from Lisa that the Indians receive free health care and that the hospital is part of the IHS (Indian Health Service) which works in a similar way to our NHS. Reuben asks Lisa, "What would happen to Dave if he had something wrong with him whilst on the reservation and needed to come here?" Lisa puts my mind at ease, well a little at least, "We would patch him up and make him stable and send him on to another hospital." That's reassuring, knowing that they would not just watch me die is something I guess.

Reuben's family are good people. I appreciate the friendly way that they have all treated me. None of them have made me feel like an outsider and it has been a pleasure to be in their company.

Arriving back in Rapid City, Reuben receives a call from Carlos. He has just got back from his 24 hours on the hill and tells Reuben about his experiences. Although I am privy to this conversation, I shall respect how private these things are and allow them to remain personal to Carlos. Reuben is extremely proud of his brother and tears well up in his eyes as they speak. The fortuitous timing of my visit allows me to witness this special moment.

As a thank you to Viv and Reuben for their hospitality over the past week, I have offered to take them for a meal this evening to show my appreciation. Earlier in the week they had mentioned an (Asian) Indian restaurant in Rapid City. Obviously, with me being English and curry being our (adopted) national dish, this would be ideal. We go straight there on our way back from Pine Ridge.

It's now early evening and the restaurant is due to close soon. It is not so much a restaurant, more a café that serves Indian food. You order at the counter and take your food to a table. It does not have the usual menu that I am used to back home, and the options are basic. I'm a little disappointed as I wanted to take Reuben and Viv for a proper meal, I felt as though they deserved more than this. However, it is just a bit of a misunderstanding and we make the most of our curry and rice.

As we eat, Reuben tells the owner of the establishment that I am from England and therefore it was paramount that we came and had a curry. The (Asian) Indian (I know, it gets a bit confusing) guy smiles and tells us that he prefers the food in London to India itself, we all laugh. I know what he means as 'English' Indian food has its own taste, although I'm not sure I agree that it's better. The food that I have eaten in Kerala, South West India, has been amazing. The meal here is good, it just lacked a bit of the experience of going to an Indian restaurant in the UK. Maybe we will be able to rectify that at a later date. If Viv and Reuben ever visit Nickey and I in England, I will make sure of it.

Back at their home, we decide to watch the film 'Snatch'. It has been mentioned a few times during the past week and we have agreed that we should watch it together. Reuben and Viv do not have a television, so I set up my laptop and we watch via Netflix. We laugh our way through the movie while enjoying a drink.

We need to be up very early the next morning as Reuben is catching a flight to New York. He has been invited to speak at a conference. I have agreed to drop him off at Rapid City airport and then take a slow trip back down to Denver, planning to stop overnight halfway. The downside is that Reuben has to be at the airport at 5:30am, this means setting the alarm for 4:30am. I get all my stuff together, ready to just take to the car as we leave.

With a heavy heart I say goodbye to Viv, as she will not be up when we leave in the morning. We hug, and I thank her for the great hospitality she has shown me. Viv is very much like Nickey, a no-nonsense, tough woman. You know exactly where you stand with Viv, and I love that. This is why the mention from both her and Reuben of adoption means so much. I am sad to be saying good bye, yet I know that it is just for now.

Time for bed.

CHAPTER TWENTY-SEVEN

FAREWELL MY FRIENDS

The alarm on my telephone rings out, it can't be 4:30 already, surely? I pick up the phone and check through squinted eyes and yes, it is. I hit the snooze button. I don't go back to sleep but try to wake myself gradually. My eyes keep wanting to close but my mind tells them to open. Just get up, I keep saying to myself...yeah, yeah, two minutes...no now...argggh... okay, okay I'm up.

Reuben taps on my door, "Are you awake Dave?"

"Yes mate, be out in two minutes," I manage to sound friendly (I hope).

I sit up, get my clothes together and head to the bathroom. A quick wash to freshen up and I'm ready to go.

We load the car and set off to the airport, a twenty-minute drive at this time of day.

Rapid City airport is only small, mostly with internal flights coming in and out. I wish that I had arranged to fly out of here to maybe New York and then directly home from there, rather than driving back to Colorado. Admittedly, I needed to fly into Denver for my meeting with Christine, but I could have made other plans for my return. We live and learn.

I pull up to the drop-off bay. We get out of the car and Reuben takes his travel bag from the back. We shake hands and hug in a similar way to when I arrived, only this time instead of joy and excitement, there is sadness.

"Have a safe trip to New York. Thank you so much for the last week," I say.

"No problem my brother. I hope you get back home safely. Say hi to Nickey for me,"

"Will do. I'll let you know when I'm back home."

Reuben heads off into the terminal and I jump back into the car. I hate goodbyes.

It is just before 5:30am and I'm now alone. I only have myself for company until I arrive back in England the day after tomorrow. I don't mind this for short spells but in general, I'm a people person and like to be in the company of others. It may be a long two days for me. However, being alone does give me time to think and reflect.

I decided a day or two ago that this would be a good opportunity, with time to kill, to pay a visit to Wall Drug. This is a large retail tourist attraction in South Dakota. On our previous visit, whilst up at Old Faithful in Yellowstone, Nickey and I purchased a pillow that has a picture of a wolf on it. Our granddaughter loves it and I thought that I may be able to get her one here, as from what I have seen, it specialises in souvenirs of this type.

When I leave Reuben, it's still dark. The sun comes up as I drive, it is fully daylight by the time I pull up outside of the drug store.

Wall Drug has a quirky little story behind it, which is the reason why it has become such an attraction. It started out as a small pharmacy, owned by Ted and Dorothy Hustead during the 1930's. Struggling for business, they came up with a novel way of attracting customers. The store lies just off-of a main highway. Many cars drove past them every day, they just needed to find a way of drawing these potential customers from the highway and into their shop. The answer they came up with was a simple one. People travelling long distances, especially in the warmer months, would always welcome a chance to stop and rehydrate. They placed big signs on the highway offering 'FREE WATER' and the customers started to come. Once they had stopped, there was every chance that they would buy other goods on offer. From here on they went from strength to strength. Well done to them.

Once off-of the highway, a sign directs me to a small road that has parking bays and shops that line it. I pull into a space close to the doors of Wall Drug. I am one of the first to arrive as they are yet to open. I plan to have breakfast here and wait hungrily to be let in. Once inside, I don't have a free water but do have a 5 cents cup of coffee (refillable obviously) with my breakfast. I think this is their modern-day version of the Free Water offer.

I finish eating and take a slow wander around. It is a large store that is partitioned into different sections. It is quite impressive for what it is, but the success story is the draw that brings people here in my opinion. The merchandise on offer is exactly as you would expect it to be, tee shirts, cuddly toys, pens, caps etc. Sadly though, amongst all of this there is no wolf pillow so I have-to buy other small gifts to take back to my family. That's me done as a tourist. Time to move on.

Today, I have planned to take a slow drive back down in the general direction of Denver. I'm going to do it the old-fashioned way and use a map instead of the satnav. Driving down through Nebraska and into Colorado, I will drive until I either see somewhere that I wish to stop, or I feel too tired to carry on.

My mood is a little strange, torn between being sad from saying goodbye to my friends and looking forward to getting home to my family. During this interim, I have the feeling of drifting without any real purpose. With the last week or so being pretty full-on, not even having a destination for the day does not seem right some-how.

A few hours into my drive, my eyes begin to feel a little heavy. With a late-ish night and an early start, along with the sun shining brightly through the windscreen, the rate at which I become tired increases. It is now close to lunchtime and I start to consider my options, as in, where might be a good place to stop for the night. I pull over into a layby and look at the map. There is a town called Scottsbluff that I should reach within the next hour, that will be my stop-over destination. It's about the halfway mark between Rapid City and Denver. That means tomorrow, hopefully after a good night sleep, I will just have the last three to four hours to drive.

As I approach Scottsbluff, the occasional buildings start to appear along the roadside. These become more frequent the further into the small town I get. Then a large Walmart with a gas station, and about half a mile on from there, a motel. That will do.

I pull off the road and park outside of the reception. The rooms are all on one level and are set out in a square around the carpark. I walk in to the reception and wait a couple of minutes for somebody to come to serve me.

A lady, similar in age to myself comes out from the back, I ask if she has any rooms available for the night and how much it would cost? They do, and it would be $50. Perfect. Cheap and cheerful is exactly what I need.

You may have noticed that I have not named this motel. There is a reason for that. Cheap it may be, cheerful it most certainly is not.

The lady picks up a key and leads me to my room. I have the one on the end, nearest the entrance/exit. She unlocks the door and opens it to reveal, what I can only describe as a prison cell. She does not hang around, which is not surprising, if I had not just paid her $50 I wouldn't have either. The dark-brown carpet has rips in it. The room is dull, and it looks like damp above the door through which I have just entered. The small window has dark-brown curtains to match the carpet, they can't have been taken down for any reason since the seventies. You would think that they would have to have removed them whilst they painted. That wouldn't have been an issue, as it clearly has not seen a paint brush since the seventies either. The television was of the big box style (you guessed it, just like in the seventies) and I feel as though I have booked a night in the room that time forgot.

This was not what I had in mind when I left Rapid City this morning. I tell myself that it is just for one night, I will have to suck it up and get on with it.

I move the car to just outside of my door and bring my bag in. I switch the television on, wondering if it is going to work, it does, so I lay on the bed watching the news. Donald Trump continues with his presidential campaign. He is in Bismarck in North Dakota making derogatory remarks about a female senator that had previously had some controversy regarding how she described her heritage, calling her 'Pocahontas'. The reporter tells how this upsets people in the Native American community as they see it as a stereotypical, racist slur. Not the best comment from somebody running for office.

I fall asleep watching the television and wake up an hour later. Now what?

As I said when writing about Pine Ridge, I believe the environment that I find myself in creeps in to my psychi. Without

171

consciously thinking about it, my impression of the town is affected by the room that I'm sat in. My desire to explore, to get out and see what's around me, is non-existent. I will have to eat something so will need to venture out of this little hell hole that I'm calling home for the night at some point. The only place that I am aware of is Walmart, which has a McDonalds inside. That will have to do for today. If I were not alone, I'm sure that I would have done all I could to get out of here for a few hours. What strange creatures we are.

As I lay here, I look back over some of my notes. I reflect on the week that has just passed. I think of a relative way of viewing this whole subject in conjunction with my visit.

I have had a great time at Reuben and Viv's and I love Rapid City. So, imagine if I were to say, "Thank you guys so much for your hospitality, I have loved my time here, I think I might stay. I know that you have given up your bedroom for me, that is very good of you. I have decided to bring Nickey over." After a few weeks of Nickey and I living in their house, we are settling in nicely. Reuben and Viv are beginning to think, "These guys are starting to out stay their welcome, but it would be rude to kick them out." They continue with their hospitality. Before they know it, we have brought our daughter, my son-in-law and my granddaughter over too. Reuben and Viv are now living in a corner of their lounge. We are larger in number and are quite forceful in making sure that we use the bathroom first and that we have the first picking of the food in the kitchen. We have effectively completely taken over their home.

To show our appreciation, we dedicate one day every year to thank them, we have family around and eat turkey. We may even let Reuben and Viv have some. That is how grateful we are.

It all sounds a bit crazy, but is that not what happened with white Europeans taking over America, yet on a scale of much greater magnitude? After-all, Nickey and I have not killed our hosts.

I fall asleep early tonight, there's not much to stay awake for. I am now very much looking forward to getting home.

I set off on the last part of my trip at about 9:30am. With the estimated driving time approximately four hours, this will give me another four hours at the airport to relax, have a drink and something to eat before boarding the flight to London. Well, at least that was my plan.

The drive is straight forward for the most part, until I reach the outskirts of Denver...then traffic. Fortunately, it's not a problem as I have given myself plenty of time.

I plod slowly on through the traffic for a while, then thankfully it starts to speed up again. For this last section of my journey I put myself back in the hands of the satnav, although I'm not so sure that it is working correctly, probably something that I have done wrong, but I have no idea what.

The satnav gives me no verbal directions, so I continue straight on the road that I'm on. I look down at it and I wonder if I should have pulled off, it's all a little confusing, however it is now giving me directions again. I follow its lead, although not convinced that it is taking me to the airport. I'm getting closer to the city and more concerned. I appear to be on a magical mystery tour. It becomes clearer that I'm on the wrong path when the satnav speaks, "You have reached your destination." There is not an aeroplane in sight. I'm now completely lost in downtown Denver. Did I mention that I hate Denver?

I have no idea how far I am from the airport, so I ask a passer-by. He tells me that I'm about 15 miles away. I need to head East.

I try to work out the satnav. I think that it has taken me to a previous command that somebody else had entered. To people that know me, it will not be a shock that I have messed up with this basic piece of technology, I'm a bit of a technophobe...well that phobia has now increased tenfold.

All the extra time that I have given myself is now dwindling. I'm beginning to panic that I could miss my plane. To make matters worse, this is a Friday evening on a holiday weekend, the disc jockey on the local radio station tells me that the traffic is getting heavy as people plan their getaways. Thanks for that.

I see a delivery man stood at the back of his van with the doors open. I pull up behind him and ask if he can direct me to the airport. This person turns out to be my saviour. He gives me simple instructions back to the main highway that would take me to my destination. Once on the highway, the signposts are more frequent and although the traffic is heavy again, I know that I'm back on track. With the stress that I have put on myself, I have decided that

I'm not going to stop to fill up with fuel, I will just pay the bill that the car hire company give me.

When I eventually arrive back at the airport, I breathe a sigh of relief. The stress that I was feeling an hour ago was pretty intense, I can now relax and reduce my anxiety. That had been an awful trip. I drive the car straight up to the drop off point to where the car hire company employee is waiting. "I haven't filled up I'm afraid," I tell the lady as she approaches me.

"Oh, okay. Did you want to go and do it quickly before I run the barcode gun over?" she replies.

"How much will it cost me if I don't?"

"For this vehicle, probably between 100 – 200 dollars."

"Wow, I wasn't expecting it to be that much. Where's the nearest gas station?"

"Literally just straight on this road, about a mile down."

I check my watch, I have enough time, "Okay, I will be back in 5 minutes."

To fill up costs me just under $30.

I have always returned my rental cars with full tanks in the past, so this has never been an issue. Fortunately, the nice lady gave me the option, otherwise it would have been an expensive lesson learned.

Making my way to check-in, I look at the time once again. I'm well behind from what I had planned. So much so that I am actually the last person to check-in...and all of the economy seats are taken. I can see an upgrade coming. This could be the tactic that does it for me. None of the 'tips' that I had read mentioned this one.

Yes, there is an upgrade made, sadly not for me. The airline upgrade one of their club members and I get the seat that has been vacated. There is still a little bit of good news, as the lucky person that is getting (as I see it) my upgrade is a member, they have one of the better seats in economy which I am now allocated. Better than nothing.

The next hour or so is spent doing the usual airport things, queueing to get through security (this took most of it), drinking coffee, looking in the shops and generally hanging around waiting.

On boarding the aeroplane, I see that I am seated at the back and where all of the other rows have three seats, my row has just two. One less seat equals a little more space. That'll do nicely.

After the day that I have had, my plan is to shut my eyes and wake up in London. The man sat next to me seems to have the same idea, although polite to each other, we barely say a word. The flight passes quickly, and we touch down back in the UK before we know it.

Nickey is waiting for me at the other side of the arrivals gate. We hug and make our way back to the car.

It's a Saturday morning, so the traffic is not heavy. On our drive back to Southampton, I attempt to tell Nickey all about it. In a conversation such as this, it's hard to get everything across. All of my experiences cannot be summed up in a car journey from London to Southampton. She will just have to read this book if she wants to know, in detail, what I got up to.

The experiences that I have had on this trip are very fresh in my mind. Have you ever experienced the feeling when somebody close to you passes away and you look at the world moving on around you as if nothing has happened and think, "Hey, what are you doing? Don't you know what has just happened?" well, I experience a similar feeling today but without the obvious grief and sadness that death brings.

I look at the people going about their business on this Spring Saturday morning and think back to where I was just a couple of days ago. We may all live on one planet yet there are many different worlds within it.

Time to get myself back into this one I guess. At least now though, I have a better understanding of the one that I have left behind.

CHAPTER TWENTY-EIGHT

SORRY

One thing that I cannot escape from is that I am a white European man, which, by association puts me on the other side. I'm from the side of the enemy. When I look at myself in the mirror, I see an honest man that wants to do all he can to help. When the Indians see me for the first time, they see something different. They are wary that I am just another in a long-line of people out to exploit them. This is why Ladonna gave me a hard time initially, why Joye could not be convinced to tell me her experiences at camp. The reason that Christine opened our meeting with questions as to my objectives.

I mentioned, whilst writing about my meeting with Ladonna, that I wanted to apologise for the things of which she spoke but never felt that saying the word 'sorry' was going to cut it. Well, that is still the case, but I'm going to attempt to anyway.

I know that Christine McCleave seeks acknowledgements of wrong doings to the Native Americans within the boarding school system. I'm going to give her that too.

The sad thing is, I'm a nobody. I am not a president, a prime minister nor a king. I am not in a position to speak for anyone else, however, I can speak for myself. I can comment because I have seen what I have seen.

Over the course of my journey, I have eaten with these people, drank with these people, travelled with these people and shared rooms with these people. I have laughed with them and even cried with them. Do you know the one fundamental difference between them and I? Every day when they wake up they face a struggle. Not because of who they are as individuals but because of who they are as a race.

So, my words to the indigenous people of America are, I am sorry.

I am sorry for the way you have been treated. I am sorry that we stole your land. I am sorry that we broke all of the treaties. I am sorry that we killed your buffalo so that your food sources were depleted. I am sorry that we introduced small pox and other diseases to your people. I am sorry that we stopped you from praying to your own God. I am sorry that we tried to kill off your languages and ultimately your way of life. I am sorry for Wounded Knee and the White Stone massacre along with all of the other mass killings. I am sorry for the 38 Dakota hangings. I am sorry for the sterilisations that took place in the 1970's. I am sorry for the boarding schools.

I am sorry for the Dakota Pipeline and the treatment that the water protectors came under whilst making a stand. I am sorry for the continued oppression. I am truly sorry for all of it.

But most of all, I am sorry that no-one in a position of power will say what I just have. That they too, are sorry.

CHAPTER TWENTY-NINE

BOUNDARIES

An observation that I have made regarding this subject is, the majority of people tend to sit on one of two sides. Firstly, you have the cowboys v Indians view, which has been portrayed through decades of Hollywood movies. Cowboys were always the good guys and Indians bad. I am of an age where, through my young childhood years, these western films were shown every Sunday afternoon on our television screens. As a young boy, I loved them. When we played 'cowboys and Indians', nobody ever wanted to be the Indian.

I now know that this is a somewhat distorted account of history. Quite simply, I, like many others, was brainwashed from an early age. Some people carry that through life with them. Others, like me, question these things and look deeper into it. We then come to our own conclusion based on the information we take in.

That is one view.

Then there are a whole other bunch of people that see it all as a lovely, romantic subject. The spiritual side of things grab their attention and they run with it. Although I can see, and totally understand the attraction, it is important that we remember one thing; Native Americans hate this. Yes, they have these wonderful traditions, ceremonies and beliefs, but they are theirs. They do not appreciate these things being hijacked by us while we turn a blind eye to their daily struggles. A post that I have seen recently on Pinterest reads...

'Funny how everybody likes the 'Indian' that talks about the earth, the water, harmony, feathers and spirit animals. But nobody likes the 'Indian' that talks about the invasion, terrorism, murder, genocide, plundering and rapes by the settlers.'

A fair point.

The best thing we could do is erase both of these views from our minds and start afresh.

I'm not saying that I have all-of the answers, far from it. All I can do is relay my experiences and the way that I have perceived them.

Recently during a conversation with my best friend in his local pub, we were discussing my writing of this book with another of the locals, somebody that I had never met before. My friend, also named Dave, asked, "Obviously, because you are writing your book, you have been well received by the Native Americans but how are others received by them?"

Unfortunately, the conversation moved on very quickly (as tends to be the case when alcohol is involved) and I never really got to answer the question. So, I will attempt to answer it now.

The reason I have been received in the way that I have has nothing to do with me writing a book. If anything, that could work against me. If I had just cold contacted people, I doubt that I would have got very far. I probably would have been met by a similar reaction to that I received from Joye Braun. This is not because they are unfriendly, they are just sceptical.

I believe that there are a couple of reasons why I have been accepted in the way I have. Firstly, by far the most important is my relationship with Reuben. The trust that I gained from him has spread to others. If he trusts me, so can they. The other reason, and probably why Reuben and I became good friends in the first place, is because I do not cross any boundaries. I totally understand my position.

It is important for us to realise that, one thing that does NOT make us allies is dressing up as them for Halloween/fancy-dress parties or using them as mascots for our sports teams. They find this highly offensive as it characterises them, increasing their struggle of getting people to realise they are still here, still fighting their battles. We also should never don a headdress or war bonnet (even fake ones). These are earned by the Native Americans that wear them and a part of their heritage that they take very seriously. So, knowing that just having an affection for their culture means nothing, it even irritates them, this leads me to a big question. If we want to be allies, what can we do?

All too often, we say things like, "what THEY need to do is...". I even found myself starting to do this earlier in the book until I stopped, checked myself and realised what I was doing. Perhaps the thing we should be saying is, "what WE need to do is...". With this we need guidance.

I have put this to some of the people that have featured throughout the book to get their take on it.

The first person to get back to me is Christine McCleave. She opens by saying that she likes what I am doing with the book and thanks me. Christine also comments on why she feels I have been received in such a way and that it is not just because Reuben trusted me, more because I went to their communities and sat with them. "I was less interested in opening up to you until I met you in person and made my own assessment about your intentions," she tells me. It pleases me to hear this.

"The best way to be a white ally is to listen to -and defer to- communities of colour. No matter how much you understand, you cannot speak for us and doing so reinforces your white privilege and the idea that your voice is more important than ours.

Privilege means that you owe a debt. You were born with it. You did not ask for it. And you did not pay for it either. No one is blaming you for having it. You are lovely, human, and amazing. Being a citizen of a society requires work from everyone within that society. It is up to you whether you choose to acknowledge the work that is yours to do. It is up to you whether you choose to pay this debt and how you choose to do so.

Sometimes living with privilege can disillusion us into thinking that being in a community with other humans does not require work. This is a lie; it requires a great deal of work. And all of that work requires being a human and trying to love other humans well.

However it looks, it will be something that you do without needing to be thanked or receive praise-you are not a saviour. Marginalized/disenfranchised folks can and will survive without you – we are magic. However, I urge you to pursue this work, knowing that a system of white privilege afforded you access to opportunities while denying them to so many others."

Whilst writing this chapter, I see a post put on Facebook by HolyElk Lafferty (we share some mutual friends) which started 'Dear white Allies', this grabs my attention and I read through it and see that it sits perfectly in this section. Her comments are aimed at 'us' becoming defensive regarding the past. I contact HolyElk to gain her permission to use it. "I would be honoured," is her response. Thank you HolyElk. So, this is her view on this topic…

'Dear white allies,

Those diamonds you see sparkling in the eyes of Indigenous women have been forged by the will to survive darkness. We've chosen to carry that shine despite living in a world that tries to beat it out of our souls every day. So, while it's a beautiful thing to watch us as we stand in our power, speak our painful stories and fight the battles we choose, remember that it's taking every ounce of strength we are made of to do that.

When you ask how you can help us, this is what we need…

Remember that often the villains in our stories are white but we're fighting in our hearts to not hate an entire race of humans because we know what that feels like. Remember that we deserve to speak our truths without having to defend and justify our feelings or worse yet…to console you. Remember that your sensitivity to our truths invalidates our reality, no matter how rational it sounds in your mind. Understand that we're trying to build bridges, but it shuts down construction when you react this way.

We've been sitting on mountains of grief and stories are waiting to be told. Let that be the hardest challenge. '

HolyElk Lafferty

HolyElk has a large facebook following and played a big part at Standing Rock. She is now actively working hard for a brighter future. As you can see, she is also very good with words.

I contact Reuben to gain his response to my question. We end up discussing it on facetime. It is the first time that we have spoken in this way. I'm of the age where technology such as this amazes me. We sit and chat for a while face to face and it costs me nothing. So, I put the question to him and let him speak...

"Over my years of being a tour guide I have seen many different outlooks on the subject. Some people come, take a look, fulfil their curiosity and then leave. Others may get tearful and apologise. I say to them the same as I have said to you Dave, you personally have done nothing wrong and have nothing to apologise for. A lot of these things happened a long time ago, way before we existed."

I counter that by saying, "but things are still happening though Reuben. I believe that we need to apologise, somebody somewhere has to take some responsibility, at the very least acknowledge what has happened and that it is still going on. If it starts with the likes of me, then so be it."

"Dave, it's good to hear you say that, I appreciate it. These apologies have been made in Canada and I believe that if they were made here, it would go a long way. Will it ever happen? I am not so sure."

Reuben tells me that he believes there is more sympathy for their cause from foreign visitors, it tends to be the white Americans that struggle with feeling any compassion. I think that may go back to what I said in the second chapter regarding their guilty conscience. At some point, it needs to be faced up to.

Later, after our conversation, Reuben sends me some links to songs by a singer called Marty Stuart. One is entitled 'So you Want To Be An Indian'. I have a brief listen, but it has a strong country feel which is not my favourite genre of music. I write back that it is a bit "too country" for me.

"It's about the words Dave."

"Oh ok, I will have another listen and pay more attention to the lyrics."

"Marty Stuart was adopted into the Lakota culture by Marvin Helper on Pine Ridge. The song speaks. Finally, someone listened to 'us'."

Then a slight crack appears in the shell that Reuben covers himself in and he continues, "People really don't care about us unless it serves their purpose." That is one of the first times that I have heard any bitterness from him regarding the way Native Americans are treated.

I disagree with him, "I feel that may be true of some but not all. I just think that others need to be shown how to care in the right way". Hence the question that has been asked.

"Hmmmmm…"

"You're not convinced? Yes, perhaps I am a bit of a fantasist. You speak from a position of realism and experience, I speak from one of blind hope and optimism…I'm sure that you are closer to the truth."

An hour or two passes with no response, then one word, "Anyway". I imagine him saying it through an exhalation of breath, resembling a sigh.

I do not continue the conversation any further as I know exactly what he means.

'Anyway' (to term a phrase), have a listen to Marty Stuart, 'So You want To Be An Indian' on Youtube and you will get a good idea of Reuben's views on my initial question.

Dakota Goodhouse is another on my list. His responses are always in depth and informative. He is extremely knowledgeable and always gives me more information than I bank on. Dakota always sends me off on a tangent. On this occasion I have summarised his comments a little, to stay on topic. He starts by explaining that not everything is always as it seems…

"I think that the first thing WE (you and I) need is education. An example of such is the American Revolution. Americans tend to think that this war was all about the issue of "no taxation, without representation," when a major motive for the war was expansion west. After King George 111 issued his Royal Proclamation barring expansion west past the Appalachian Mountains. Colonists wanted to expand, especially those who finished indentured service and those who owned plantations, those who stood to gain from expansion.

The best thing WE (you and I as individuals) need is to accept each other. America is a land of tolerance. Tolerance lets things like hate rhetoric survive and spread. We tolerate each other, perhaps never knowing what it is we are tolerating. I think it's like drinking alcohol or taking drugs though because WE (humanity) build up a tolerance to the point we need more to provoke us to feel and act.

The best thing WE (as citizens of nations) need is to engage in social issues. This might be as simple as stepping in on someone's hate rhetoric or as volunteering at a soup kitchen now and then. This might be as active as giving money to first nations' colleges and universities for scholarships, books and facilities. Maybe actively recruit a native for a position in one's company or business. There are too many state and federal agencies that want to work with natives, yet never employ natives."

Some of Dakota's comments are aimed more at Americans than white people in general but an interesting concept nonetheless.

I am grateful for all of these comments. We now have some guidelines to work to.

CHAPTER THIRTY

A TALE OF TWO JOURNEYS

The writing of this book has had me on two journeys. The obvious one is the journey into Native America of which the whole story is based. The second is the actual writing of a book. The highs and the lows. The feeling of elation when something goes well, and I receive positive feedback, the thoughts of 'what's the point?' when I have a crisis of confidence. Sometimes I read back over my work and think it's great. Other times I'm not so sure. The importance of my mission drives me on anyway.

I have dedicated 3 years of my life to writing this. On a daily basis, you would find me in the 'Lunch Lounge' (the café in the business park where my gym is situated) sat in front of my computer tapping away on the keyboard. My mind drifting off to thousands of miles away, reliving my time in Indian country. When I was at school, my teachers would always say that I was a daydreamer, as if it was a bad thing. Well, now I have turned that skill into a positive. It's serving me well.

Many hours between clients and training is spent writing. "Have you not finished that book yet?" I get asked regularly by the other patrons of the cafe that are aware of my project… and looks from the others, as if to say, "are you in here again?"

We are now sadly coming to the end of our journey together. This does not mean that, as a whole it is over, just this part. You may decide that you would like to find out more, on the other hand this may be enough to satisfy your curiosity on this subject. Either way, that is fine. All I hope is that you have enjoyed the ride. That you have learnt something that you didn't already know. Most of all, that you now realise that Native America is not just dream catchers and proverbs. There is a struggle that has been going on for hundreds of years… and continues, on a daily basis.

Before we part company and go our separate ways, I would like to give an update on the lives of some of the people that have played major roles in my story. Over this past three years, I have learnt a lot, however, on the surface, my life has mostly stayed the same. This cannot be said for a lot of the new friends that I have made along the way.

Firstly, I have to tell you that, through the duration of the protests at Standing Rock, Reuben and Viv separated. After which, Viv became very involved in the whole movement and spent most of her time at the camp. When the camp ceased to exist, Viv headed to Alaska to stay with some old friends that she had met up with during the protests. She has now made it a more permanent move. I keep up with Viv via social media. Her son Charlie is now married and has recently had a child.

The fact that Viv and Reuben are no longer together does not dampen my feelings towards her. I like Viv a lot and have very fond memories of the time that I spent with her. It is not for me to make judgements as to what caused their split or even to ask. It is not my business. I just wish them both happy lives.

After the split, Reuben moved to Pine Ridge where he cared for his mother. Sadly, she passed away a few months later. It was very sad to hear this news, I am proud to have had the privilege of meeting her. Mavis was a genuinely lovely lady that will be missed by many.

Reuben's life then drifted for a while until he met a new love, Susie Schmeider, whom he has now moved to New York City to live with. Reuben and I speak regularly. Nickey and I are planning to visit him in the future. They are also invited to visit us in England anytime they wish. It will be nice to reverse roles and for me to be his guide.

Darren remains in Rapid City. His career just seems to keep going from strength to strength. Throughout the pipeline protests, Darren wrote many articles and done a lot of media work. He also played his music at benefit concerts. He continues to perform at the Crazy Horse monument and has recently released his third CD. Every time I see Darren on Facebook, he has another amazing announcement. The sky is the limit for this man.

Carlos successfully took part in the Sundance. I am aware that it is not for me to write too much about the spiritual side of his experience, but I can say how it was as a personal sense of achievement for him. I have asked if he can share anything with me that would not be too intrusive. Did it change his outlook on life?

"Yes, it did, tremendously. I realised that we have a connection to Tunkasila (the creator). Closer than you would think. He is always there when you let him be. And Tunkasila is good, he's full of love. It's hard to describe the feeling in words but the closest way I can is to compare it to the love grandparents have for their grandchildren. They love them so much, they almost can't do anything wrong. But, if they do, and then ask forgiveness, of course, it is given. I walk today with a confidence that I am not alone, I never was. And that my late parents are in good company. I'll see them again and all who passed over when it's my time."

Carlos tells me that he had dreamt of doing a Sundance years before, and to actually achieve it is great, "but it goes much deeper than that. I wish I could tell you more." Carlos stays respectful to the whole process by limiting what he says. "What I can tell you is that I was a part of something much bigger. It's very powerful and wakan (holy), I respect it, so that is as far as I can go I'm afraid."

I'm grateful to him for sharing as much as he has, I understand this reserved approach and believe it is the right way for him to act. Without pushing the boundaries, I ask one more question; if he has, or would, do it again? "I have done it again and I will continue to pray for those I love, my family and friends, and the people, forever."

Christine McCleave, from the Boarding School Healing Coalition, moved back to Mineapolis with her family. At least, if I ever have the pleasure of meeting up with her again, I will not have to concern myself with getting lost in Denver. Christine continues her undeniably invaluable work of gaining peace and healing for her people through the Boarding School Healing Coalition. I hope that sales of this book will assist her in some way.

Tipiziwin and her husband, Ti Tolman, from the Immersion Nest at Sitting Bull College have moved their family to Washington to further their education.

The Immersion Nest continues in the capable hands of Yuliya Manyakina. Once again, let's hope that we can make a difference to them too.

I also have some news on White Clay. If you remember from the second chapter, White Clay is the place in Nebraska, just a couple of miles outside of Pine Ridge. The place where many Native Americans would purchase their alcohol.

The shops of White Clay have lost their liquor licenses. My initial response to this was one of joy, but when I think a little more about it, I wonder if it is a good thing? It really does no more than place a plaster (or band aid if you are American) on a gaping wound. It does not cure the problem, far from it, all it does is moves it. These people are still addicted, now they will just need to source their fix from elsewhere. With Pine Ridge still being dry, my guess is it will just create more underground activity.

Hopefully these things have been considered and a long-term plan is in place to address them.

I think that wraps up most of it, which just leaves me. My life has, for the most of it, remained the same throughout this project. Perhaps the changes are about to come, who knows? Something I have learnt throughout this is, you just don't know what is around the next corner.

There is, however, just one small difference that I would like to add before my final word…I can now finally be introduced as, "Dave Jones from South-Hampton. He *is* an English author."

One thing that I would like to do before I sign off, and that is to thank each and every one of you for purchasing a copy of this book. By doing so, with all of the profits from sales going to Indian charities, you have contributed in trying to make a difference, and for that, I thank you with all my heart.

THE END

SPECIAL THANKS

I would like to thank all of you that came along for the ride. No readers = no book.

To everybody that has helped in any slight way with this, I cannot thank you enough. Without your participation, this would not have happened. To all of the Native Americans that spared me their time and told me their stories, I know that I had to win some of your trust. I am happy that you gave me the benefits of your doubts. To the people back home that gave me their views on snippets that I read to them. Thank you. To my good friend Michele Capel, that had the difficult task of editing the whole thing, you helped turn this into a book. And another friend, Sally James, for designing the cover. My father, who gave some valuable advice early on. Also, to both of my parents for raising me to be a person that cares. I remember when I was young my father boycotted South African goods. I had no concept of apartheid, I could not understand why we would not buy the juiciest apples in the supermarket. Well now I understand. My grandfather, who sadly passed away in 2014 at the age of 93, an old war hero that our family are very proud of. The money that he left me paid for our initial trip. I know this would make him happy.

To the people that gave me words of encouragement. Thank you.

Nickey deserves a huge mention. Her support has been immense. I must have been difficult to be around when my confidence was low, but she always built me back up. I also have to thank her for giving me her blessing to return for part two…even though she saw it as just another holiday.

The biggest thank you has to go to my Lakota brother, Reuben FastHorse. He opened so many doors for me. He had a one hundred percent belief in me from the day he read the first chapter literally just after I had written it. Although there are thousands of miles between us, we shall always be close. Philamayaye Khola (thank you friend).

I dedicate this poem to Reuben...

THE FEATHERS I HAVE WITHIN

I have visited your reservations, paid my respects at Wounded Knee,
I may be an observer, yet I never just came to see.
An Englishman on a journey, is all I claim to be,
But the story of your people, has had an affect on me.

I may not have Lakota blood, I may have pure white skin,
But my heart it beats just as yours, for the feathers I have within.

You opened up your life to me, you shared with me your home,
Introduced your friends and family, took me to the Camp Of The
Scared Stone.
A whole new world my eyes can see, for now I have been shown,
A blessing our meeting might just be, now we shall never walk
alone.

I may not have Lakota blood, I may have pure white skin,
But my heart it beats just as yours, for the feathers I have within.

DAVE JONES

The eagle wing prior to being made in to a beautiful fan

Reuben, Viv and Darren at the Sitting Bull monument

Dakota GoodHouse and I just before unravelling the winter counts

The bison hide winter count

Reuben entertaining the water protectors at the camp

Carlos and I before he heads up on the hill